RECLAIMING A PASSION FOR WHAT ENDURES

ETERNITY

JOSEPH M. STOWELL

MOODY PRESS

CHICAGO

ISBN: 0-8024-4152-1

3 5 7 9 10 8 6 4

Printed in the United States of America

*With enduring gratitude to
my Lord and Savior, Jesus the Christ,
whose assurance of a better,
more enduring world beyond
makes this book worth writing,
life worth living,
and dying gain*

CONTENTS

SETTING
THE STAGE

Paul Azinger was at the height of his professional golf career when the doctor told him that he had life-threatening cancer. Up to that moment he had not given much thought to dying. Life was too all-consuming for him to stop and consider the reality of the grave and all that is beyond. But that encounter with the inevitability of eternity was an abrupt reality check. His life would never again be the same. Even the $1.46 million he had made as a professional golfer that year paled to insignificance. All he could think about was what the the chaplain of the tour had said: "We think that we are in the land of the living going to the land of the dying when in reality we are in the land of the dying headed for the land of the living."

Embracing the reality of the world to come radically alters everything in this world. Our values are prioritized and purified. Money, things, time, friends, enemies, family, and life itself are all adjusted to their appropriate worth and place.

If anyone should express the reality of eternity, it's those of us who have been guaranteed safe passage to the other side through

Christ, our divine passport. Yet, interestingly, we who are marked with heaven in our hearts usually live as though it were real but irrelevant. We are consumed with the tyranny of the temporal, and both the character and power of a life with an eternal focus are traded for the ordinary.

We are not unlike the average person on the street who lives out his existence in the limited confines of a one-world point of view. Blinded to the reality of the world beyond, his all-consuming expectation is to experience maximum pleasure and prosperity here. Quality of life is measured in terms of accumulating stacks of stuff and ascending to platforms of power and position. Life is defined by eating this world's best food and drinking its best wines. Leisure and large doses of comfort shape the pursuit. Finding maximum peace and the thrill of maximum pleasure become an illusive quest—illusive because ultimately this world is, at best, a hollow experience and, at worst, leaves us disillusioned and in despair. When eternity is off the screen, all of life is compressed into the distorted assumption that this is all we have. And, frankly, it's never quite enough.

Why? Because we are built for eternity. We are built for an eternal, unhindered relationship with God, who created us to know the deep pleasure of His companionship. But sin altered the landscape and forced these innate longings to search this fallen planet for satisfaction instead. Our best experiences are only feeble experiments in futile attempts to regain paradise lost.

Thankfully, redemption has put us back in touch with the eternal world beyond and has placed eternity in our hearts. Saving grace has blown down the walls that obscured our view of eternity and has given us a present relationship with Christ the King of eternity, who now lives within.

If you sense that you are missing something—that you had expected more—then perhaps you have neglected the pressing preeminence of the world to come and its first-wave expression in the person of the King who dwells in the world that is in our hearts. It is only when we actively embrace the world beyond and the world within in their proper perspectives that we become capable of finally coping with and conquering our fleeting experience in this present world.

Eternity welcomes you to the expanded perspectives of the world to come, the privileges of living in the light of a new, redeemed world within, and the real nature of this temporal, fading world that looms larger than it should on the horizon of our existence. No life, no experience can be all that it is intended without an accurate understanding and application of the dynamics of all these worlds.

*　　　*　　　*

I am deeply indebted to many who assisted me in the process of putting this material into your hands:

My wife, Martie, who encouraged me and endured the distraction of this project with grace and patience

Lori Imhof, my secretary, who cleared the decks for me more than once so that I could be free to work on this project without interruption

Beth Longjohn, whose tireless work on draft after draft and whose insights and editorial adjustments were indispensable

Jim Vincent, Cheryl Dunlop, Linda Holland, Joe O'Day, and others on the editorial staff at Moody Press

Peggy Noonan, whose seminal thoughts on eternity gave birth in my heart to a passion for this material

*　　　*　　　*

May God bless you with the pleasure of a life that is lived with eternity clearly in view.

PART ONE
IN OTHER WORLDS

Life is most disappointing, most despairing, when it is lived as though this world is all we have. Questions have few answers, and crises become all-consuming. Thankfully, this is not the only world. Christ connects us to the eternal world to come and provides for us an eternally redeemed world within. This present world makes sense only when we live here in light of these other worlds.

As Paul said, "If we have hoped in Christ in this life only, we are of all men most to be pitied" (1 Cor. 15:19).

CHAPTER ONE

BEYOND OURSELVES

A WORLD OUT OF SYNC

The Willises are an average family—average, that is, except for the fact that they have been blessed with nine children. Duane "Scott" Willis, forty-seven, is a schoolteacher and part-time minister in the Mount Greenwood neighborhood on the south side of Chicago. You've never seen his name in lights, listened to him on the radio, or picked up a book with *Willis* on the spine. But that's never been important to him. What has been important is his love for his children and his wife, Janet, and faithfulness to his Lord.

Scott and Janet have an unusually strong commitment to their children. Their three oldest children have flown the nest, and Janet has home-schooled Ben, thirteen; Joe, eleven; Sam, nine; Hank, seven; and Elizabeth, three. Peter, at only six weeks, was the newest member of the family. Much of who they were as a family revolved around raising their children. Like most families they have kept busy with school, work, Little League, and local park district activities where Scott served as coach and cheerleader for his boys. Unspoiled by the greed of the shallow world around them, they happily and contentedly have given themselves to the few things that really count—rearing their family and tending the flock at church. Quite frankly, these kinds of people are my heroes.

Recently Scott, Janet, and six of their nine children climbed into their new van to drive north of Milwaukee to visit one of their older children. That day would not be just like any other day for the Willis family. As they continued north on the interstate that skirts the west side of Milwaukee, a large piece of metal fell from a truck in front of them, piercing the underside of their fuel tank and igniting the gas. Immediately flames engulfed their van. On fire, Scott and Janet tumbled from the van. After rolling on the grassy knoll to extinguish the flames, they stared back at the roadway. All but one of their children were still inside the van. The inferno had entombed five of their children; the sixth would die the next morning in the hospital. Janet cried out in anguish, "No! No!" Scott tried to comfort her. But the children were gone.

This devastating event in Scott and Janet's world reminds us afresh that there is something wrong . . . something unsettlingly out of sync in our world. Why them? Why then? Why would God give them a desire for children and the joy of a full quiver, and then suddenly snatch them away? And why, in a world full of neglectful and abusive parents, would God permit this to happen to a family with such qualified and concerned parents?

And, quite frankly, we wonder why God would allow this to happen to His own. It seems an embarrassment to His divine character. Fairness, justice, mercy, and love all come into question in moments like these. An event such as this threatens to erode our confidence in God. It shakes the foundations of our faith.

When I was in elementary school, my teacher once distributed pictures that were full of inconsistencies and contradictions. Across the top of each picture the words "What's Wrong with This Picture?" challenged us to identify the discrepancies, which upon close observation became obvious: a boy with no eyes on his face, a dog with no tail, a squirrel taking a bird bath.

SOMETHING IS WRONG

You don't have to look long to see that something seems dreadfully wrong with the Willises' picture.

Granted, the story of Scott and Janet is unusually tragic, the kind that few of us will ever face. Yet their tragedy reminds us that our own lives are full of dissonance and disappointments that unsettle our faith and trust.

Inequities abound in our imperfect world. Consider those who through no fault of their own have been abused—individuals who have grown up in unsafe, violent environments. And how can we justify the fact that some children who've grown up in godly homes break their parents' hearts by pursuing destructive, rebellious lifestyles? What of wayward parents who shatter the serenity and crush the dreams of their children? Or what about the faithful pastor who spends his entire life in a small, unknown ministry with little income or fame? And what of the fact that he may work harder and even be more faithful to his Lord than others who land in bigger, better, and more comfortable places of ministry? Why has God rewarded him so slightly when others have so much?

Or think of those who have claimed Christ as Lord of their lives yet, instead of increased peace and pleasure, face problems and challenges for their commitment. Or why is it that those of us who want to experience a deeper, more intimate relationship with Him even in the best of moments find that there is a distance that keeps our hearts from being finally, fully, and completely satisfied? And what of those times when He seems so silent, so far away?

What about common, good folk who just never seem to win at the lottery of life? Who struggle more than bad people and have far less than many who manipulate and use their power and prosperity to advance that which is not good?

Why do the righteous so often struggle and suffer when the wicked seem to prosper?

All of us can list the times and ways that unsettling, seemingly unanswerable questions like these have challenged our faith.

Everything seemed out of sync to me on that day before I was to preach at the memorial service for one of the great missionary statesmen of our time. My struggle did not relate to the fact that he died; that's a given for all of us. It was *how* and *when* that seemed so very wrong. Phil Armstrong, who as a young man gave his life to Christ and then rose to leadership in the Far Eastern Gospel Crusade, was broadly recognized for his gifts and contributions to global evangelism. I remember as a seminarian sitting under Phil's ministry and being challenged by his message and impressed with his life. Quite frankly, I was surprised that I now had the privilege of being his pastor. Though he was traveling most of the time on mission business, I can still remember his wise input and counsel in board meetings and his personal encouragement to me in those early days when I felt insecure and wondered whether or not I would be able to shepherd that rather high-profile flock.

He and his wife, Bobbie, had dreamed about the day that his ministry load would be reduced and he would step away from mission leadership and do those few things for Christ that he really loved to do. For Bobbie this meant finally having more time with her husband. She had given him to the cause of Christ for decades of their married life, all with the hope and dream that someday they would buy a little place in the North Carolina mountains and enjoy each other more fully in their twilight years. And now, as Phil was approaching the time when he would step down from his executive directorship of the mission, they had picked out the place where their dreams would be realized.

I'll never forget that September morning during Sunday school when we received word that the small plane Phil had been flying in across the Alaskan ocean had disappeared in the night and had not yet been found in those dark, cold waters. We called Bobbie out of her Sunday school class and shared the hard news with her. Little did we know that in the days to come the party would eventually abandon its search without finding either the plane or Phil.

And now, with family, close friends, and ministry leaders gathering from across the country, it became my task to somehow find the right words to put all of this in perspective. It was a tough assignment, given the fact that there seemed to be so much wrong with the picture.

FAITH ON THE LINE

Life has a way of driving our faith dangerously close to the edge. What we expect from God so often seems to contradict what we experience in life. We find ourselves wanting to ask, *If God is good, then why? If God is all-powerful, then where is He now? If God loves me, then why aren't I happier? Richer? Why don't I have fewer problems and more peace? If God is pleased with me, why don't I experience more pleasure?*

Unanswered questions like these threaten our enthusiasm and heartfelt commitment to Christ. We find our faith growing more stoic, our view of God less emotive. We develop a kind of Christianity that shrugs its shoulders and says, *Well, that's just the way it is,* and since the stakes are too high to deny God, we just decide to buck up, grin, bear it, and hope that no one ever asks us these kinds of questions. In fact, we may even come to believe that in order to maintain spiritual sanity we need to park our brains and questions outside the door of faith and separate the spiritual realm from the realities of life. At this point faith itself becomes unreal and irrelevant.

We are left to slug it out on our own, believing that the only relevant resources are in this present world.

A disintegrating faith creates a resigned, despairing Christianity that lacks vibrancy and enthusiasm for God and His Word. Our edge is dulled, leaving us passionless and pessimistic. This decline of confidence in and commitment to God may be why there is something dreadfully wrong and out of sync with *us.*

When faith doesn't make sense and this world becomes our only reality and resource, greed consumes us, leaving us disenfranchised from generosity toward those in need and ministries that advance the cause of Christ. It leaves us vulnerable to harboring ongoing, sometimes lifelong bitterness. It may have something to do with the fact that we seem to be involved in such a frantic search for happiness—here and now—and feel disappointed when we don't find it. A fallen faith leaves us vulnerable to the unending pursuit of pleasure and prosperity. Believing that the only real world is this world, our careers are viewed by most of us as merely platforms upon which we can establish our own sense of significance, build our own kingdoms, and secure safety and security for ourselves in the present world.

Our disorientation is compounded as we search the Scriptures only to discover that throughout the ages our world has been out of sync and filled with contradictions. In earliest times Job suffered in horrendous proportions for no apparent earthly good; Joseph was thrown into the slammer for three years for being righteous; prophets were killed by God's own people; God came to live among us and was crucified; and the blood of the martyrs has stained the soil for centuries.

SOMETHING BEYOND OURSELVES

Yet these and a multitude of others rose above their out-of-sync world with an unshakable confidence in a sustaining divine presence within and a better, more blessed world beyond this one.

When Janet Willis looked back toward the burning minivan and cried out "No! No!" her husband's comfort was more than just a touch. He had a perspective beyond the moment—indeed, beyond this world. Scott touched her shoulder with his blistered hand and whispered, "Janet, this is what we've been prepared for. Janet, it was quick, and they're with the Lord."

Clearly Scott was in touch with something beyond this present world.

In a front-page story the *Chicago Tribune* reported, "Burned, bandaged, and still in physical pain in a Milwaukee area hospital, the couple displayed extraordinary grace and courage Wednesday as they calmly presided over a news conference they had requested to tell of how their unquestioning belief has sustained them through the loss of six of their nine children." At the news conference Scott said, "I know God has purposes and God has reasons. . . . God has demonstrated His love to us and our family. There is no question in our mind that God is good, and we praise Him in all things."[1]

Could it be that *our* faith has not yet grown big enough to embrace something of significance beyond ourselves? Beyond this present world? Could it be that we expect Him to give us the best of all worlds in this world?

The fault is not with God. It is with us; we have assumed that this world should be a pleasant and friendly place and that the answers to the troublesome questions of life can be found in the temporal realm. We have assumed that the answers to life's dilemmas lie somewhere within us, among us, or within the realm of the immediate world around us. We are wrong.

The questions are ours. But the answers are often found in the perspectives of the world beyond.

We have assumed as well that solutions to our enigmas can be forged in this single, flat, earthbound existence. We are wrong.

The problems are ours. The solutions lie beyond ourselves.

Stanton is a small English village that dates back to the thirteenth century. At its center stands the Church of St. Michael's and All the Angels. Inside this time-worn house of worship are burial markers in the floor and on the walls, memorializing the faithful who have gone on from there. On one intriguing plaque, mounted just to the right of the pulpit, is this statement, etched for all to note:

> Sacred to the memory of Frances, third daughter of Reginald and Frances Wynniatt, who died March 12, 1808, aged 19 years. Cut off in the morning of life her many amiable virtues had endeared her to all who knew her. Sensible and prudent in all her actions she lived unspotted from the world and untainted from any of its vanities. . . . Upheld by the animating prospect of a future and a better state of existence, she supported the lingering illness, which brought her to a premature grave with exemplary patience and cheerful resignation.

Frances Wynniatt was a woman who found her strength and confidence in something beyond herself—in something beyond her world.

CHAPTER TWO

IN OTHER WORLDS

AN EXPANDED POINT OF VIEW

Some of you will remember when 3-D comics and movies were all the rage. To bring the picture into focus you had to wear the right eyewear—glasses composed of cardboard frames with orange cellophane lenses. Without the glasses the picture was blurry and nonsensical, but with them the picture became clear and meaningful and compellingly real. Moviegoers would scream as monsters leaped from the screen, and their stomachs would be in their throats on the roller coaster. If our whole perspective lacks an expanded point of view and is limited to this present world, then distortion will always disorient both life and faith.

Peggy Noonan, former correspondent with CBS News and speechwriter for presidents Reagan and Bush, insightfully observes:

> I think we have lost the old knowledge that happiness is overrated—that, in a way, life is overrated. We have lost, somehow, a sense of mystery—about us, our purpose, our meaning, our role. Our ancestors believed in two worlds, and understood this to be

the solitary, poor, nasty, brutish and short one. We are the first generation of man that actually expected to find happiness here on earth, and our search for it has caused such unhappiness. The reason: If you do not believe in another, higher world, if you believe only in the flat material world around you, if you believe that this is your only chance at happiness—if that is what you believe, then you are not disappointed when the world does not give you a good measure of its riches, you are despairing.[1]

When the apostle Paul wrote that if only in this life we have faith in Christ, we are of all men most to be pitied (1 Cor. 15:19), he was on to a very important truth. If this is the only world for us, then the misery of a passive pessimism is indeed our lot. In this statement Paul has given us a hint as to what may be wrong with our picture. Could it be that our frame of reference has been locked into this world only? The Bible indicates that there are, in fact, not two worlds as Noonan notes, but *three* worlds that are both real and relevant? When life with all its joys and sorrows is viewed through the broader perspectives of these other worlds, our spiritual passions reignite and our faith satisfies all unanswered questions.

Scripture crafts biblical eyewear with lenses that bring life into focus, integrating the three distinct worlds to which every believer belongs. This biblical prescription orients us to the *world to come* . . . the eternal world of heaven; the *world within* . . . the kingdom of Christ where He reigns as King over the realm of our lives and seeks to express the values, attitudes, and reactions of His kingdom through us; and the *world around us* . . . this present, hollow, fallen, temporal world.

WORLDLY WISDOM

What are the characteristics of these worlds? The *world around us* tends toward unfairness, danger, and disappointment, and ultimately it will leave us unsatisfied and disappointed. It is a world controlled by our adversary. Its intrinsic nature is temporal. Filled with the qualities of our good and loving God, *the world to come,* on the other hand, is characterized by limitless satisfaction and joy. And the redemptive *world within* is equipped to be a victorious, first-wave expression of our final experience in eternity. The believer is called to see all of life in the context of these three distinct spheres.

Paul Harvey's series, "The Rest of the Story," intriguingly relates real-life situations that are seemingly enigmatic and unanswerable. Then, after the final commercial break, he comes back and tells "the rest of the story." As the final details unfold, the earlier information comes into focus and makes sense. Similarly, with all three worlds in clear view, we can see life in its fullest meaning.

If all we have is this world, then revenge, bitterness, and hatred will be our response when deep injustices come upon us. If, however, we understand that this world is prone to offense and cruelty but that in the world to come God will guarantee that every wrong will be made right and that justice will be done, we are suddenly released from the pressure of dealing with the issue ourselves. Yielding the tension to God for His care, we can be free emotionally, psychologically, and spiritually to love even our offenders. This is exactly what Paul commands that we do in Romans 12 where he says that we are not to render evil for evil, but to put wrath in its proper place. That proper place is at the throne of God who lives today in heaven and sees all that transpires on this earth. Knowing, then, that God will deal from the world beyond with our enemies, we are free to respond in peace. If our enemies are hungry we can feed them, or if they're thirsty we can give them to drink (Rom. 12:17–21).

Those without Christ have only this present world as their frame of reference. The world beyond is either denied or largely unnoticed. For them the world within is merely an extension of the fallen world to which they have become enslaved. That is why a life without a relationship with the King of eternity and with no confidence of a fulfilling existence in eternity is at best hollow and at worst desperate.

We of all people should be neither hollow nor desperate. Sir Fred Catherwood, a former vice president of the European Parliament who was knighted for public service, writes in an article entitled "Before It's Too Late":

> British Society has gone badly wrong. You don't just have to look at the terrible statistics. People have started to look back to the

good old days—not so long ago—when the streets were safe, everyone had a job, most people had a home, children stayed at school, the family stayed together and we all looked forward to better times. We look back today because we dare not look forward. We live in a violent, greedy, rootless, cynical, and hopeless society and we don't know what's to become of it all.[2]

You might think he was writing about America. Catherwood cites causes for the decline. The first one he states is greed, which he calls "the logical result of the belief that there is no life after death. We grab what we can while we can however we can and then hold on to it hard." He goes on to note that having lost sight of the God of eternity, society is motivated by what is personally expedient. "The powerful use their power and the weak go to the wall, not just the poor, but the weak-willed, and especially all the children, who depend on the age-old disciplines and loving care of the family. As we stop believing in the dignity of man and woman made in the image of God, violence has risen dramatically."[3]

Yet, this present world often captures our attention and distracts us from our focus on the world to come and the impulses of the kingdom within, leading to disappointing consequences. In fact, most of the regrets of our lives come from failing to embrace eternity as a consuming, motivational reality and failing to align our lives to the values of the kingdom.

Greed offers us nothing more than the empty shell of things that cannot satisfy. Our preoccupation with our own advancement breeds tension, trauma, and sometimes tragedy in our most prized relationships. Our clamor for earth-side power and prestige preempts the time, energy, and attention that we could give to our children, our spouses, and the less fortunate. Instead, we trade the values of the kingdom and an assured, eternal reward for a moment in the spotlight.

In hindsight, we can look back and realize that most of our lives have been poured into the bottomless bucket of this world, and that, after all is said and done, the bucket is still empty. Worse yet, imagine stepping onto the shore on the other side and realizing that we have brought nothing with us of eternal worth. Think of looking into the face of our eternal God, realizing that our lives reflect only earth-side existence rather than the meaningful, profound realities of the kingdom. In eternity our hearts may echo the words of John Greenleaf Whittier, "For all sad words of tongue or pen, the saddest are these: 'It might have been.'"

How then do we as believers actively embrace the reality of all the worlds to which we belong? First, we learn the sequence. There are many events in life where sequence is everything. As we often say, it is important to keep first things first. It's important that national anthems be sung before games begin. That appetizers precede entrées. That engagement comes before marriage. And that crawling happens before walking. It is the same with understanding the worlds to which we belong. When embracing the reality of these worlds, sequence is everything.

FIRST THINGS FIRST

Eternity is primary. Heaven must become our first and ultimate point of reference. We are built for it, redeemed for it, and on our way to it. Success demands that we see and respond to *now* in the light of *then.* All that we have, are, and accumulate must be seen as resources by which we can influence and impact the world beyond. Even our tragedies are viewed as events that can bring eternal gain.

Second, while living in light of the world to come, our lives in the here and now are to be directed by the authority of the King who lives within us. Instead of being absorbed by misdirected values and trends of this present world, we are redeemed to express the values and realities of His kingdom to the watching world around us.

Once we embrace in sequence the eternal world beyond and the eternal world within, we are ready to face the world around us realistically and triumphantly. This present world is a place created by God for His glory, His gain, and our enjoyment. But it is a place corrupted by the Fall and crowded with a fallen race. It is a place under the dominion of Satan who is bent on defacing and defaming God and His glory. The world around us is a dangerous and destructive environment that, when left to itself, creates tension and trouble.

Unfortunately, instead of a steady biblical expression of the sequence of these three elements of a believer's existence, we tend to move in and out of these worlds in a random fashion. Given the particular pressures of the moment, we periodically prioritize, ignore, forget, and reclaim their significance.

For instance, we are often pressed with the reality of eternity only when a loved one dies. Or when we grow old and begin to realize that most of life has passed and we note with regret the little we have done for eternity, the little we will take with us there, and the short time left to do much of significance for heaven's sake. Most of us live as though this world is where we are rewarded, and happiness, satisfaction, fulfillment, and prosperity not only can be ours here and now but should be.

The understanding that we have been delivered from the domain of Satan and transplanted into the kingdom of His dear Son escapes us. We seem unaware—or worse, uninterested—in the unique values of the kingdom of Christ and the fact that we are called to be an advance announcement of eternity. We remain unaware until we are confronted by a stirring sermon or perhaps a failure in life that graphically brings to light the fact that we have not responded to Him as King but have sought to manage and maneuver our own way through life for our own benefit and gain. When the sermon has faded and the failure has been reconciled, we quickly slip back into building our own kingdoms here and now.

If heaven is our consistent hope and the King is our guide and the expression of His kingdom is our calling, then life in this world comes more clearly into view. Its disappointments don't damage or surprise us. We expect little of it, for our reward is yet to come, and we hope to take captives from it in our march toward home.

In short, the blending of these worlds means that we live confidently *here* in the light of *there*, reflecting the culture and values of the *kingdom within* under the authority of the King.

Henry Ford, the great automobile magnate, was advised by some of his colleagues at the Ford Motor Company to hire a consultant to solve some of the problems created by the phenomenal growth of the car industry. Reluctantly, since Ford never liked to spend money, he hired a consultant by the name of Steinmetz. When Steinmetz's work was done he sent Henry Ford a bill for $10,000—a huge sum of money in Ford's day. Ford was outraged. According to correspondence on display at the Henry Ford Museum, he wrote back to Steinmetz expressing his shock and disappointment at the cost of the consultation and requesting that Steinmetz send him a detailed invoice itemizing the details of the consultation. In this correspondence Ford said, "This is an outrageous charge for just tinkering around."

Steinmetz wrote back that he was pleased to provide a detailed accounting of the cost. The itemized invoice stated $10 for tinkering around and $9,990 for knowing where to tinker.

Our problem is not that we don't spend time tinkering around with our Christianity. We have simply not known *where* to tinker. Knowing how to maximize our faith is not a complicated concept. It always involves the realization that we are redeemed for something far beyond ourselves, our time, our space, and our history. And that within us are planted the beginning seeds of the world to come, the indwelling King, and our commitment to the values and expressions of eternity.

Redemption has liberated us to citizenship in another world, with an insightful view of this present world and fortified by a redeemed world within. We are called to clearly view the reality of this present world, embrace the world beyond, and live by the instincts of the resurrected world within.

SEEING CLEARLY

Martin Luther saw this present world clearly when he wrote, "This world with devils filled should threaten to undo us." If we are not careful we can forget that we live in a fallen place in the midst of a fallen race. As one scholar has insightfully noted, if we understood the depth of the Fall we would be surprised that anything good could possibly ever happen to us on this earth. The world around us is the domain of our adversary, and we are not exempt from the effects of this place. Isaac Watts, in his penetrating hymn "Am I a Soldier of the Cross?" wrote:

> Am I a soldier of the cross,
>   a follower of the Lamb,
>   and shall I fear to own His cause,
>   or blush to speak His name?
> Must I be carried to the skies
>   on flowery beds of ease,

> while others fought to win the prize,
> and sailed through bloody seas?
> Are there no foes for me to face?
> Must I not stem the flood?
> Is this vile world a friend to grace,
> to help me on to God?
> Sure, I must fight if I would reign;
> increase my courage, Lord;
> I'll bear the toil, endure the pain,
> supported by Thy Word.

But not only must we see the world around us clearly, we must look far enough ahead, fully embracing the reality of the world to come.

While most all of us would like to embrace the reality of the world to come, for many it seems neither *real* nor *relevant*. The vast majority of Christians live no differently than the pagans who believe "You only go around once, so get all you can." We have somehow forgotten that heaven transforms our lives in this world. In fact, our actions become radically, wonderfully re-arranged when heaven comes clearly into view. It's only when we lift our eyes to heaven that life and its faith-threatening questions take on new significance. Heaven must be more than a spiritual fantasy land, a divine Disney World in the sky. It must be our transforming point of reference.

The resurrection of Christ and His post-resurrection appearances gave the apostles a keen sense of the reality of the world to come. It was this reality that empowered, energized, and defined the New Testament church as a force with which this world could not reckon. Because heaven was real they would not be seduced by the lesser things of this world. They viewed the threat of death as simply the door to all that is better.

Having seen the reality of our world clearly and embracing the world to come leaves only a surrender to the redemptive world within to complete our reorientation. While being a Christian is a privilege that we appreciate, we often fail to accept the realities and responsibilities of the fact that the King reigns within—that we are His and He is ours, and that at our very essence we are children of His kingdom. For some reason we still live as though our lives were our own to be managed and maneuvered by our passions, pride, and the promptings of our instincts. We fail to recognize that the culture of the kingdom has been planted within our hearts and, as such, we are called to express the values, attitudes, actions, and reactions characteristic of the kingdom to come.

PERSPECTIVES FROM THE OTHER SIDE

Refusing to live only for this present, brutish world enables us to come to grips with the transforming realities of the three worlds to which we belong. Bringing them into sync will give perspective to both pain and pleasure, gain and giving, suffering and satisfaction, heartache and happiness. It will rekindle a passion in our spirit that can sustain us just as it did the early Christians. A three-world perspective reassures us, even in the midst of pain or confusion, that God is good and life is well worth living. When we come to grips with the world around us, the world beyond us, and the world within us, we sense a revived faith, no longer quarantined by the questions of life. A three-world orientation motivates our spirits to undaunted service to Him.

In a lead editorial, the *Chicago Tribune* heralded the strength of the Willises' faith by quoting Scott as saying, "I must tell you, we hurt and sorrow as you parents would for your children. The depth of pain is indescribable. The Bible expresses our feelings that we sorrow, but not as those without hope." The writer of the editorial continued, "Hope is founded in faith and in the conviction, in Janet Willis's words, that 'He is the giver and the taker of life and He sustains us.'"[4] Janet and Scott are clearly in touch with the redemptive world within while aware of the short, nasty, brutish world around them. If for them life was defined by this present world alone, the devastation would have been overwhelming.

Living in and viewing all of life from other worlds, the Willises were able to transform their tragedy to His glory. Knowing that this world offers no guarantees of safety, security, and satisfaction, the Willises had cultivated an unshakable confidence in the King who lives within and ultimately brings all things to His glory. They were clearly oriented to the truth that all of life was to be seen in light of the world to come. And it was that perspective that the Willises portrayed to a watching world—to every major media outlet in the Midwest—a compelling victory over this present world, anchored in a firm embrace of the world to come and a full surrender to the King of the world within them.

It is this other-world point of view that prompted Scott to declare, "Janet and I have had to realize that we're not taking the short view of life. We take the long view and that includes eternal life."[5]

It's no wonder that the *Tribune* editorial concluded, "There are only two possible responses to the kind of loss that Duane and Janet Willis suffered last week: utter despair or unquestioning faith. For the Willises, despair was never an option."[6]

CHAPTER THREE

BALANCING OUR WORLDS

CHRISTIANITY OUT OF SYNC

In 1864, when she was thirty years old, Hetty Green inherited her father's fortune of $1 million. She bought Civil War bonds when others spurned them, and in a short time she became a multimillionaire.

Yet she lived like a pauper. Hetty worked alone at a bank, and for lunch she'd pull a ham sandwich from her grubby pocket. When her son was injured in a sledding accident, Hetty tried to get free treatment at a charity ward, but she was recognized and charged. Unwilling to pay, she treated the wound herself. It festered, and her son's leg had to be amputated. Ironically, at her death, Hetty Green's estate was worth more than $100 million.[1]

As strange as her way of living may seem, our own lives often reflect the same dynamics. Having been redeemed, we continue to focus on the scant resources of this hollow world. We fail to recognize the wealth of our redemption and to embrace the treasures of the world within and our inheritance in the world beyond. We live as though redemption has changed nothing, and we view our existence in the narrow realm of this present world. It's not that we don't believe this is a fallen place; nor do we deny that heaven is real and will be ours someday; nor do we deny that He is King. It's just that we still *live* as though none of it were relevant, and as a result, we share the same delusion and disappointment of the pagan. We question if our faith gives us any advantage after all. More tragically, we diminish our ability to be effective light in the darkness, salt on this earth. We offer no compelling reasons why others should look to Him as Lord and Savior of their eternity since our lives too often reflect the flat and disappointing perspectives of this world.

Yet a more subtle and prevalent distortion is embracing all three worlds and implementing their ramifications in an unbalanced way.

BENT TOWARD EARTH

The most prevalent distortion is displayed by the *earthbound believer.* Earthbound Christians live the important segments of their lives only in the context of this world. Their expectations, dreams, plans, hopes, and schemes relate to what they can acquire and experience now. Money, careers, family, retirement, and time are managed and manipulated by the tyranny of *temporalism.* Those in this category are far more susceptible to greed, the pursuit of immediate peace and pleasure, and a success that is defined by competence and credentials that enhance our own sense of significance.

Since eternity is not our guide, concepts like investing in the world to come have little influence on us. We give out of a sense of obedience and obligation. We see our careers as platforms for our own significance and security, not as a means to advance the eternal kingdom of Christ or as a platform upon which to stage the values of the King. Obedience to the point of discomfort, loss, or suffering is an unthinkable option since we have been trained to expect peace, satisfaction, and emotional fulfillment here on earth.

Since the philosophical underpinnings of our generation both deny the existence of God and reject the values of His righteous kingdom, we are content to sing about heaven, to hear sermons about the authority of Christ and the values of His kingdom, but we fail *here* in the light of *there.* We have enshrined this world and its offerings and relegated our other worlds to some kind of religious fantasy.

STARRY-EYED SAINTS

Not all of us, however, are of this earthbound group. Another distortion of the worlds to which we belong involves those believers who have turned their backs on this world to focus solely on the world to come and the reality of an ultimate kingdom where God will rule. Earth for these *heaven-only* types is a naughty, damnable place, waiting for its ultimate destruction.

To these individuals material things are not only suspect but intrinsically evil. Involvement in the material world is seen only as a necessary requirement for survival. Cocooning in clusters formed by our own families and the community of fellow believers, there is little impetus that turns our hearts back toward this fallen place. We have no interest in invading this fallen place with torches held high to make a difference in the lives of those who are lost and dying in this world. We fail to see that this earth, though fallen, is still the created order of God for which we are in some measure responsible and which we can still use to glorify His name and advance His cause. Sinners, particularly the most obvious, are viewed as those who will get what they deserve rather than candidates for heaven, objects of a compassionate, dying, bleeding Savior who sacrificed Himself for even the least of these on this planet.

Heaven-only folk become so heavenly minded that they are of little earthly good, and as such they project to a watching world an image that is not only unattractive but unattainable. The extremes cluster in communes waiting for the return of the Lord. But a more prevalent expression is reflected in our propensity to cloister ourselves in our comfortable communities of belief with no God-centered focus on our careers, material possessions, wealth, environment, and with no compassion toward those in the world; particularly those who engineer and promote agendas that promote unrighteousness. Consumed in our churches, we have no presence in our communities. All that is secular is "endured." Only the "sacred" is significant. But a proper understanding of our worlds would see all of life as a sacred experience.

This heaven-only perspective is often a by-product of the structures of our faith. Since the community of believers is a key priority; since the values we live by make mixing with our world uncomfortable; since we tend to become consumed with the support and maintenance of kingdom institutions with their needs, codes of conduct, committees, commitments, and programs, we are left with little time, energy, or interest to fulfill our biblical assignments in this world. Ironically, our absorption in kingdom work here often loses sight of the fact that we should be doing all we are doing for the sake of eternity and for gain of His kingdom. We easily succumb to doing church work to maintain the work for the work's sake and may even stoop to do it for our own glory and gain.

FOR THE BEAUTY OF THE EARTH

Some of us distort our three-world calling in exactly the opposite way. By discounting the significance of the long view of eternity and the ultimate doom of this world, we focus efforts in kingdom terms on this present world. *Kingdom-on-earth* types sense that their calling is to bring the remediating power of kingdom values to neighborhoods, cities, and social structures. While giving lip service to the redemptive value of lost souls, in practice they give the vast bulk of their energies and resources toward the betterment of this planet with little thought of eternal gain. They tend to be content when parents become more responsible, health clinics open to meet medical needs in impoverished neighborhoods, stomachs are filled, and people are steered toward a more self-sufficient, non-welfare posture. And while all of this is done in the name of God and His kingdom, you can tell that something is out of sync when there is little emphasis on the gospel and a clear presentation of Christ's redemptive work to reconcile those they serve to Christ Himself as Savior. This kind of nearsightedness views eternity dimly and rallies its resources to earth-side causes, consuming the energy and resources that should be finally focused on eternity's gain. We may in this imbalance become politically correct, sociologically relevant, even celebrated—but ineffective in an eternal perspective. We may feel fulfilled and satisfied having spent ourselves in these arenas with little or no eternal gain, but we are out of sync.

Of course, earth-side agendas are important from a biblical perspective. Yet if we dispense cups of cold water but not in His name and not toward the meaning of His eternal redemptive goals, then we are out of balance. Building houses with no reference to eternal homes; filling stomachs and leaving hearts still hungry for God; making life better with no reference to eternal life; reorienting lives to society without orienting them toward God; reconciling the races without reconciling lives to the Creator of the races are all temporal pursuits and ultimately contribute little to eternal significance.

THEOLOGICAL CORRECTNESS

Some of this imbalance may be born out of the pressures we face to respond to the many social agendas platformed in our culture. Issues that relate to environment, race, economics, and quality of life are the right target for concern if I am a sensitive and correct member of this society. For the living-now-in-the-light-of-there-under-the-authority-of-the-King believer, issues like these resonate in our souls. What sets us apart, however, is the fact that we do not respond to these realities because it is the "thing to do" but rather because we are driven by the theology of our kingdom values. Our focus on racial issues, for instance, finds its impetus in God's creation of all of us in His image and the obvious reality that Christ in His love and compassion embraces all of us as precious. Environmental issues relate to our stewardship of God's creation that allows the earth to reflect His glory. Social justice finds its impetus in our belief in a God who is just. Articulating clearly why we do what we do in earth-side agendas and using our efforts to point those who observe us to the God who motivates us is important in terms of our commitment to communicating the values of our King and the certainty of eternity.

Living in a city like Chicago, I am constantly aware of these kinds of concerns. Whether it be an environmental issue like air quality or societal tragedies like homelessness, abuse, crime, racial tension, social injustice, etc., it is impossible to ignore their presence and their pain. As such, many ministries in Chicago focus on offering both help and healing. Several balanced ministries blend their concern for the world around us and clearly state their allegiance to the values of the eternal kingdom, and as quickly as possible move all the way to needs that are eternal. Circle Urban Ministries, under the direction of Glenn Kehrein, a white, and Raleigh Washington, a black, demonstrates the loving care of Christ to Chicago's near-west Austin community, one of the most dangerous and despairing communities in Chicago. They express the compassion of Christ through medical clinics, housing renovation projects, job training, and counseling. In connection with the Rock of Our Salvation Church which Raleigh pastors, the ministry is unashamedly involved in moving from physical compassion to spiritual compassion, and it shares effectively the realities of Christ. Today throughout the Austin community many people have settled their eternal destination, having all that is far better to look forward to, because Circle Urban Ministries (CUM) has embraced all three worlds to which God has called them, and it functions in the biblical cadence of that call.

City officials have begun to notice the change in the neighborhood as well as in its residents. Chicago mayor Richard Daley has proclaimed CUM's work a model in our city. What has happened is that CUM has looked beyond fleeting cultural agendas to eternal kingdom values, and over the years it has created a vibrant testimony to the glory of God.

FOR CHRIST'S SAKE

Throughout the last couple of centuries Bible-believing Christians have led the way in terms of this eternal commitment to earth-side concerns. In the nineteenth century English evangelicals led the fight to abolish slave trade. Leading ministers such as Charles Haddon Spurgeon and George Müeller opened orphanages to house street children in an environment where they would not only be safe and secure, but where they would learn the good news of Jesus Christ as well. Rescue missions in our major cities have touched the down-and-outers with the compassion of Christ. They have effectively ministered to the physical needs of people while glorifying God and populating heaven as well. Here in Chicago the Pacific Garden Mission has modeled this since 1877. To this day it continues to carry out a ministry that reflects the balance of the three worlds to which it is committed.

One of our fine employees at Moody is a model product of worlds in balance. He works on the staff of our Solheim Center for Urban Outreach and Physical Education. But John Sanders was not always a productive, joy-filled person. At age sixteen he moved to the south side of Chicago to live with his older brother. The only thing that promised meaning for him was the world of drugs where sin had addicted him to its power. This led, inevitably, to a life of crime to support his drug habit, and John served three terms in prison. Cops on the beat knew John and often told him that he was hopeless and that he would ultimately die in prison. In the depths of John's heart, he believed they were right. One day, cold and broke, John stumbled into the Pacific Garden Mission where he could get earth-side warmth and nourishment. There he heard about the God of eternity who loved and died for him. Eventually John gave his heart to the Lord, who gave John a whole new perspective—not just on life, but on life lived in the light of eternity. The power of redemption broke his addiction and enabled him, with the encouragement of fellow believers, to begin a new, productive, and fulfilling life.

Similar stories echo from places like the south side of Chicago to the posh suburban neighborhoods. Lives dedicated to serving the cause of eternity in the midst of this nasty world are used by God to launch rescues that focus on people whose needs are not just present but eternal as well.

Ministries that focus on results like these are worthy of our support. When thinking of investing time and resources in these three-world-balanced ministries, some key questions to ask are: (1) How do they program for follow-up and evangelism? (2) What connections does the ministry have with a local church? (3) Can they point to converts who are growing in Christ and recycling themselves into the work of the kingdom?

PARISH POLITICS

One of the most seductive forces in this *kingdom-on-earth* disorientation is the politicizing of the church in the last couple decades. This well-meaning effort to change society politically reflects a debilitating imbalance. Most of us think that if we had the right political influence—a messianic presence in the Oval Office and Christians on Capitol Hill—we could restore this fallen earth to its intended redemptive peace. And while as citizens we ought to work to influence a righteous society and to hold our government accountable for righteous practices, the church's main thrust is not political revolution but redemptive influence. Homes, neighborhoods, and schools will not be healed and crime-free until lives are changed through Christ and the values of the kingdom are lived out on a regular basis. Counting on political processes to accomplish our goals has politicized our King (would Christ really be a right-wing Republican if He were here?) and undermined the eternal cause of the gospel. We have confused the message of the Cross and the meaning of the kingdom with political agendas, and thus we have distorted the reality of Christ in both this world and the world to come.

FOLLOWING CHRIST'S EXAMPLE

It is noteworthy that Jesus pointed His disciples toward an accurate expression of life here in light of the world that He was leading them toward. The disciples, in fact, illustrate our tendency to get these three worlds out of sync.

The disciples had strong earthbound impulses. In Luke 12 they were distracted from the reality of eternity by being anxious for what they would eat and what they would wear. Christ warned them not to be consumed by temporal concerns. He called them to a broader perspective when He said,

> And do not set your heart on what you will eat or drink; do not worry about it. For the pagan world runs after all such things, and your Father knows that you need them. But seek his kingdom, and these things will be given to you as well. . . . For where your treasure is, there your heart will be also. (Luke 12:29–31, 34 NIV)

It is clear they lacked an understanding of kingdom values when they shooed the children from Christ's feet and when they were shocked that Christ would care about people like the woman at the well, who was neither politically nor morally correct from their point of view. He gave them an eternal perspective when He responded, "Let the children alone, and do not hinder them from coming to Me; for the kingdom of heaven belongs to such as these" (Matt. 19:14). And the woman at the well—this person whom no earthbound rabbi would talk to—He rescued her from this fallen place and guaranteed her a place in the world to come, and then commanded His disciples to labor for the harvest (John 4:1–42).

The disciples reflected a kingdom-here view as they continually expected the messianic ministry to remediate their earthside plight by overthrowing the oppressive regime of the Roman Empire and establishing Christ as King on earth *now* and restoring Israel to its former glory. Even after the Resurrection, the disciples questioned Jesus regarding whether this was the time for the kingdom to be established on earth. He deferred their hopes to a time that only God knew and called them to be effective on this earth in terms of winning people to a secured eternity in heaven (Acts 1:1–8).

RELIGIOUSLY WRONG

The three major religious groups in Christ's day reflected the imbalances that we are so prone toward today. The Pharisees were so caught up with their codes of behavior and the maintenance of their own power, prestige, and glory, that they gave little theological or rhetorical attention to heaven and the world to come. The Sadducees, on the other hand, comprised the religious aristocracy. They were affluent and comfortable and did not believe in the world to come. In their minds they had heaven *here* and no need of heaven *there*. The Essenes rejected the validity of this world altogether, cloistering themselves in catacombs to wait for the Messiah, lest they be corrupted and influenced by the world around them. As such they had little interest in or influence on the world around them.

Could it be that Satan has always known that denial of truth about the earth, the kingdom, and heaven would be unnecessary if he could simply, more easily, imbalance and disorient us?

CHRIST'S WORLDS IN PLAIN VIEW

When Christ came to earth as God in flesh (Emmanuel, "God with us"), He brought earth, the world within, and heaven into clear focus. Through His life and ministry He modeled the appropriate order of all three worlds. He came from *heaven* and knew that it was both real and relevant. It was His home. It was where He belonged. He made it clear that He was headed ultimately back there, and that He would endure all that is here for the joy that would be His there when His Father would restore again His glory. As John notes, He pitched His tent among us (John 1:14) and lived here in light of the real world to come.

Christ expected little from this world or its people. He knew they were fallen and needy, and He came not expecting this world to serve Him but rather that He would serve the world. He knew that it would be hostile to Him, His cause, and His message; yet He was willing to endure its discomfort and distress and even its death so that He could conquer the fallen kingdom and guarantee that the kingdom of God would reign eternally and supremely with no rival and no threat (see 1 Cor. 15:20–28).

And when He was here He taught us kingdom values. He modeled what it looks like to be a kingdom person interacting with this fallen world. He embodied a clear expression of what it means to belong to the kingdom of God. He taught His disciples to mirror the life of the kingdom to come.

When His disciples asked Him to teach them to pray, Christ again unveiled the three-world orientation of His life. He began with a clear focus on His Father who is in heaven. He revealed His passion for the kingdom that would finally and ultimately come, and that the kingdom would be an expression of His Father's will here on earth. He recognized in the prayer that life in this world is challenging and needs to be sustained by God. He recognized that there would be treachery in relationships where we would offend and be offended and that we would be seduced to finding fault in others. And then His prayer resonated with the affirmation of God's ultimate victory: "For Thine is the kingdom, and the power, and the glory" beyond this moment and beyond our time into eternity "forever. Amen" (Matt. 6:13).

At the heart of His life on this earth was the reality of eternity and heaven. Even a casual reading of the gospels reveals His preoccupation with eternity. Heaven was His home. Heaven was His all-consuming point of reference.

Heaven must also be our consuming point of reference as we seek to effectively interact with the three worlds to which we belong. We are called and redeemed to live here in the light of there, reflecting the values of the eternal kingdom of God in the earth-side places that we inhabit.

CHAPTER FOUR

LIFE IN THE LONG VIEW

CRITICAL CHOICES

What does it mean to live *here* in the light of *there?*

Living in a way that reflects our eternal destiny transforms our ambitions and actions into dynamics that this world often cannot comprehend.

Solomon wrote in the book of Ecclesiastes: "I have seen the task which God has given the sons of men with which to occupy themselves. He has . . . set eternity in their heart" (3:10–11).

Living in the light of eternity produces courage and strength. It enables us to make choices that dramatically affect all of life. Some of these decisions are quiet and unseen, receiving little attention and attracting no controversy.

At other times, eternal choices will shake life to its foundation.

Such a choice was required of a woman named Vibia Perpetua. Although she lived just two centuries after the time of Christ, in many ways she was just like any woman today. She had a husband and a newborn baby. They were new believers, members in the struggling, persecuted church of North Africa. Vibia Perpetua was just one young woman. Yet, standing up to the powers of Rome, she made a courageous choice that reflected her unshaken belief in eternity.

Linda Holland tells Vibia's story in a chapter from her recent book *Alabaster Doves.* Here it is.

Temples crowned the hilltops, jutting up from the paved streets of Carthage that wound in and out around the palace. Working-class families settled in mud-walled hovels in the suburbs, while well-to-do citizens made their homes in lavish settings in the center of town. In the open squares wealthy Roman ladies and gentlemen mingled as farmers moved through the streets carting their harvest. In the marketplace, women bearing wicker baskets bartered with proprietors for the best of the day's produce and fish.

The clip-clop of horses' hooves on the stone street signaled the crowd of approaching Roman legionnaires. People dashed from the center of the street, leaving a path for the equestrian procession, as three soldiers bearing the insignia of the proconsul pranced their steeds into the center of the marketplace and reared to a stop. The lead soldier unrolled a scroll, and holding it before him, shouted a decree:

"Ye men of Carthage, be it known to you that the divine Imperator has commanded that all men everywhere be loyal citizens. There has arisen in the Empire a superstition endangering the peace, prosperity, and happiness of our subjects. Be it known to you that throughout our land ignorant fellows have made a god of a malefactor condemned by Roman law. They are despisers of our laws. They will not sacrifice to throne and crown. For years, in patience, we have waited that these childish people might return to the obedience due the state, but they refuse, and so we now decree that they be brought to judgment.

"You are commanded that wherever you may find them to take and hold them, and to bring them to the consul. Let it be done. Farewell."

He rerolled the scroll, and the legionnaires left the marketplace with the same pomp with which they had arrived.

Meanwhile, outside of town, a young mother and her husband have joined other new members of their church by the lake. Today, they are to be baptized as new believers of Christ. Vibia Perpetua nestled her newborn son in one arm, as she and her husband watched silently and waited for their turn to enter the water, publicly professing their conversion. Vibia's face glowed with the hope of her new faith. At twenty-two, though, she couldn't have known that her commitment would demand of her the ultimate test.

Carthage, where Vibia lived, was in North Africa, where Christians from Rome had brought the Gospel and where many new Christian churches were springing up. In fact, two cornerstones of Greek and Roman paganism had been so won to Christ that North Africa had become the most advanced region of Christendom.

Already, Vibia's ties with the world were strong. She was young and beautiful, of noble birth, and well educated.

Vibia and her husband were part of the rapid growth of Christianity in North Africa. This trend alarmed the pagans. Prejudice and superstition swept the population, who demanded enforcement of obsolete laws they could use against these Christians. Responding to pressure from a few influential people, Roman Emperor Septimius Severus issued an edict prohibiting Jews and Christians alike from converting or making converts. Roman procurator Hilarianus attended fanatically to the execution of this edict in North Africa.

And so the infant church of Christ entered the martyr age. Men, women, and children were torn from their homes, judged to be dangerous citizens, and condemned to die. The jails were full of them. Executions took place daily. But certain Christians were set aside for show—for those days when killing was considered a spectacle worth watching. Defenseless Christians going to battle with wild beasts and armed gladiators had, for pagans, quickly become the preferred sporting event.

But in spite of this persecution, spiritual passion increased and the Gospel spread, creating small congregations that secretly gathered in homes to worship together. Vibia and her husband met with their group of new believers each week.

But spies lurked in the neighborhoods, reporting the names of those who gathered. Rumors spread of Vibia's baptism, and she and her husband were named among the new Christians.

Vibia's father received word from an informer that his daughter and her friends would be arrested. He ran to warn Vibia and to plead with her to renounce her faith.

Well aware of his deep love for her, Vibia was touched by his mournful pleas. And she pitied him, for he was growing old. How could she make him understand?

"Father," she tried to explain, "do you see this vessel lying here? Can one call anything by any other name than what it is?"

She paused, giving him a chance to calm himself. Then she continued, "So neither can I call myself anything else than what I am—a Christian."

Panicked by the implications of his daughter's conviction, he raged and threatened to beat her. But Vibia remained calm and firm. She had caught a glimpse of Christ's sufferings on the cross, and she was not afraid.

The next day guards appeared at Vibia's home. They burst through the front door, grabbed Vibia and her husband, their newborn baby, and Felicitas, their maidservant who was in her eighth month of pregnancy. The guards took them to the proconsul.

The blush of childhood had not yet left Vibia's face. But it began to fade to pale as the guards ushered them into the great judgment hall and before the seat of the proconsul. Vibia was thrust to the center of the room and left standing alone to face her accuser.

She stood trembling, staring down at the marble floor beneath her. The proconsul gazed reluctantly at this beautiful woman who stood before him. He had no taste for these new duties, but found himself forced to carry out a law that for decades had lain dormant on the books. He had done his best in each case to persuade the Christians to believe privately as they wished while publicly renouncing their faith to save their own lives.

As the proconsul looked down at Vibia, he began, "Young woman, you are reported to be a Christian."

Vibia raised her face to meet his eyes.

"Are you a Christian?" he demanded.

"Yes, I am a Christian," Vibia confessed shyly.

"Come now, child," he ordered, "Think as you like, but do as you are told. Take this incense from the hands of the priest and place it on the altar before the statue of our emperor."

"I cannot do that," Vibia replied, looking straight into the governor's eyes, more confident this time. "I am a Christian."

"Don't waste my time, foolish girl," he snapped. "Do as you are told!"

Vibia's husband broke loose from the guard's grasp and bolted toward her. The guard sprang after him. "My dearest, you will kill yourself, and you will kill me too," her husband pleaded, his hands reaching toward her as the guard dragged him back to the side.

Vibia turned to look at him. "My husband," she began to cry, "I will do anything you ask me to do except this. My Lord is my Master."

And turning to face the governor again, she repeated, "I am a Christian. I cannot do that."

The proconsul was speechless in the face of such a fearless confession. But Romans considered life cheap—the individual nothing, the state everything. He had no choice but to find Vibia guilty of disloyalty to the emperor.

Her husband, unable to endure such a grave test of his young faith, quickly stepped forward to renounce Christianity. Vibia's eyes widened as she watched him light the sacrificial incense and place it on the altar of the emperor. Sobbing, he fled the amphitheater.

Vibia and Felicitas were thrown into prison.

"I was very much afraid," Vibia wrote, "because I had never experienced such gloom. Fearful heat because of the crowd and from the jostling of the soldiers! Finally I was racked with anxiety for my infant."

Vibia's father and mother succeeded in getting Vibia and Felicitas placed in a better section of the prison, where they brought her infant son to her. Vibia wrote:

> I suckled my child, who was already weak. In my anxiety for him
> I spoke to my mother and brother and commended to their care
> my son. And I pined excessively because I saw them pining away
> because of me. These anxieties I suffered for many days; and I

then obtained leave that my child should remain with me in the prison. Immediately I gained strength and being relieved from my anxiety about the child, my prison suddenly became to me a palace.

Vibia's father came to the prison again to plead with his daughter. With tears in his eyes, he kissed her hands and fell at her feet. "Do not cut us off entirely," he sobbed, "for not one of us will ever hold up his head again if anything happens to you." Distressed at his sadness, Vibia tried to comfort him. But he would not be comforted.

Vibia, though, had other concerns as well. Felicitas, eight months pregnant, was worried that she might be left behind to suffer in the company of strangers instead of with her friends, for an expectant mother was not punished in public. Three days before they were to enter the arena of wild beasts, Vibia and her friends prayed that Felicitas would deliver her baby. Their prayers were answered. Felicitas's labor came a month early. As she screamed with the final pains of birth, a prison guard taunted her with, "If you cry out now, what will you do when you are thrown to the beasts?"

Finally, though, Felicitas held her beautiful daughter. Looking down at the miracle in her arms, she assured her, "I will not suffer, but Another inside me will suffer for me, because I am to suffer for Him." And she prayed that this tiny girl would grow to love Christ too. But within minutes, Felicitas was forced to make her premature farewell to her daughter before giving her to the care of her sister.

During the next day, both Felicitas and Vibia became even more conscious of their closeness to God. But they couldn't help questioning what the day ahead might bring. Unnerved by the wait, Vibia prayed and asked God to reveal their fate to her in a dream. The next day, she told her companions:

> Last night in a dream, I saw a golden ladder of wondrous size reaching up to heaven; so narrow that only one could go up at once. On its sides were every kind of iron instrument, swords, lances, hooks, daggers. If one went up carelessly, one's flesh would be torn, and pieces would be left on the iron implements. Under the ladder was a dragon of wondrous size, which laid snares for those climbing it, and frightened them from the ascent.

Saturus went up first. He had given himself up voluntarily after our arrest on our account, because he had taught us the faith, and he had not been present on the occasion of our trial. When he had reached the top of the ladder he turned and said to me, "Vibia, I am waiting for you; but take care that the dragon does not bite you." And I said, "In the name of Jesus Christ he shall not hurt me." The dragon, as if afraid of me, slowly thrust his head underneath the ladder and I trod upon his head, as if I were treading on the first step.

Vibia also told of seeing a large garden nearby. In the garden an old shepherd milked ewes. Around him stood a crowd of people dressed in white. "He gave us cheese," she told them, "and as we tasted it, the people in white said 'Amen.' The sound of their voices awakened me."

On the day before their execution, Vibia's father, worn out with worry, came one last time to plead with her. But Vibia would not change her mind. "This will be done on that scaffold which God has willed," she told her father, "for know that we have not been placed in our own power but in God's."

Vibia and her friends prepared to die—now concerned only with their own worthiness to suffer for Christ. For their last meal, instead of the feast usually given to condemned prisoners, they shared an agape—a simple religious meal, celebrating Christ's death and their love for each other. And they prayed they would have the courage to stand boldly in the face of death.

That night Vibia's baby was brought to her one last time. She held his tiny face to her breast as she soothed him with a lullaby. But he showed no interest in nursing, and Vibia's milk seemed to have dried up. So Vibia just cuddled her son as she committed his future to her Father in heaven. And she thought of her husband, as she had so many times, asking her Father to guide him down the treacherous path of questioning and grief.

The next day guards led Vibia and her companions, Felicitas, Saturninus, Revocatus, and their teacher, Saturus, into an amphitheater filled with blood-thirsty people. But before they entered the amphitheater they were led before Hilarianus, Procurator of Carthage, who was to question them. He was enthroned on the judgment seat on a platform opposite stone bleachers. Vibia stood alone in the center of the platform, facing Hilarianus, as the crowd begged for blood.

"Are you a Christian?" Hilarianus demanded.

"I am," Vibia answered. "I cannot forsake my faith for freedom. I *will* not do it. For Christ is my life, and death to me is gain."

When Vibia's father heard these words he knew that Vibia would be thrown to the beasts. In a frantic, final attempt to rescue his daughter from certain death, he ran onto the platform and grabbed Vibia to escape with her. But the guards detained him and brought him before the procurator. Hilarianus ordered the guards to take him away and beat him. Vibia's heart broke for her father. But she could not turn back.

Hilarianus signaled the executioners, who herded Vibia and her friends to the entrance of the arena to await their turn for execution.

The men—Saturus, Saturninus, and Revocatus—entered first. They were ordered to run the gauntlet between the gladiators, who were drawn up in two ranks. The men ran the gauntlet. Saturninus was immediately beheaded, but Saturus and Revocatus, severely gashed by their executioners' swords, survived this first phase of the event. The two men, covered with blood, stumbled around, stunned by the blows. The crowd, reveling in the sight of fresh blood, shouted, "Now they are baptized!"

Hunters released a leopard, a bear, and a wild boar to finish the task.

Vibia and Felicitas huddled together, sheltering their eyes from the horror. And they comforted each other with reminders that soon they would be in the arms of their Lord.

"I love you, my dear friend," Vibia said, looking intently into Felicitas's eyes. "Don't be afraid. Christ will accompany us as we enter the arena."

Clinging tightly to each other, they whispered a final prayer for courage. . . . Now it was their turn to enter the arena. The guards grabbed Vibia and Felicitas, pulling them apart from their embrace, and thrust them into the entrance of the arena. The spectators' screams swelled to a crescendo at the sight of the two women.

Vibia and Felicitas gathered their courage and, with their faces radiating an unseen Presence, began singing a psalm. Wearing a simple tunic and with her hair falling softly over her shoulders, Vibia walked into the arena. Behind her Felicitas followed.

Vibia and her friends met their deaths on a March day in A.D. 203. Assisted by wild predators and gladiators' swords, they stepped into the loving arms of their Lord.

The blood and tears of these lovers of Christ were not wasted, though. They moistened the ground into which new seed would fall and produce a harvest for Christ's kingdom. Christianity continued to grow, and many people were drawn to a faith that produced such devotion.

In her short years, Vibia learned a lesson that requires a lifetime of lessons for most of us. Vibia learned that Christ is life, death is gain.[1]

Vibia's love for Christ and the certainty of her eternal destiny meant that the things of this world no longer took priority. Facing certain death at the age of twenty-two, she chose to be faithful to her king and her eternity rather than deny her Lord for the comforts of this present, fleeting world.

PART TWO

THE ETERNAL WORLD BEYOND

It's fascinating that the most important, most strategic, most enduring place in the universe gets so little attention. The moon and Mars get more press than heaven. Yet heaven is of unrivaled significance. When we stretch our view of life to embrace its reality, all of life is wonderfully rearranged.

CHAPTER FIVE

PREOCCUPIED WITH PARADISE

HOOKING OUR HOPE ON HEAVEN

In *The Screwtape Letters,* a fanciful look at the strategies of Satan and his demons, a senior demon named Screwtape declares to his apprentice Wormwood that one way to undermine the follower of Christ is to weaken the church. "One of our great allies at present is the Church itself," Screwtape writes. "Do not misunderstand me. I do not mean the Church as we see her spread out through all time and space and rooted in eternity, terrible as an army with banners. That, I confess, is a spectacle which makes our boldest tempters uneasy."[1]

Screwtape and his comrades of darkness would have little to feel uneasy about in regard to the church today. It is hardly as terrible as "an army with banners . . . rooted in eternity." Instead, eternity for many of us holds little relevance to our everyday affairs. We live as though it is theologically real but irrelevant. In fact, one of the reasons we fail to impact our world may be that for a long time heaven has seemed unimportant to us personally and has nearly disappeared from our liturgy, sermons, hymns, prayers, thoughts, dialogue, and writing.

More than fifty years ago, the famous Scottish theologian John Baillie wrote about a decline in warnings "against the flames of hell" and about "a future day of reckoning." He urged preachers to dwell on "the joys of the heavenly rest" and to describe "the world that now is as a place of sojourn or pilgrimage."[2]

In an article on death in *The Westminster Dictionary of Christian Theology,* Paul Badham reported that "neither the medieval emphasis on fear of death nor the confident hopes of the early Christians are much in evidence today. . . . Though few churchmen explicitly repudiate belief in a future life, the virtual absence of references to it in modern hymns, prayers, and popular apologetic indicates how little part it plays in the contemporary Christian consciousness."[3]

HEAVEN ON EARTH?

As we race toward the close of the twentieth century, most of the emphasis in Christianity is on becoming happier here, healed here, more blessed here, and more fulfilled here. Worship must excite our spirits, sermons must entertain and enthrall our minds, music must penetrate and propel us. And our counseling must make us feel better about ourselves and strengthen our human bond of friendship and family. While this may be nice and necessary, without heaven in clear view our Christianity fails to have a heavenward compulsion pulling us closer to God, closer to eternity, closer to home. It tends to become instead self-serving entertainment or a therapeutic center. A heavenless church seeks to satisfy longings and needs here rather than serving and sacrificing here with a view to satisfaction there.

Without an eternal transcendent God as our compelling force and heaven in clear view, self becomes the center of attention and increasingly the center of our universe.

Noting this imbalance, A. J. Conyers observes:

> The center of life is outside our personal experience: it finds its center in God, not in the individual or in the world itself.
>
> This means that the whole structure of being, for those who seek heaven, implies a reaching out, or a reaching forward, to that which is outside the self. It is the realization that life is not essentially self-expression, but grace; it is dependent upon and focuses upon that which is beyond and outside.[4]

In a community that is not gripped by the reality of heaven, even the gospel becomes increasingly therapeutic as a means to help *feel* forgiven and restored. In fact, new adherents to the faith often expect great earth-side blessings as a result of finding Jesus as fulfiller, healer, helper, and friend . . . which of course, He is. But unless we focus our hopes on the ultimate healing that is fully experienced in eternity, disillusionment sets in as the pilgrims experience seasons of hardship and struggle.

THIS WORLD IS NOT MY HOME

We rarely see follow-up courses for new believers emphasizing the reality of heaven as our home and our identity as aliens and strangers in this world? Most, if not all, of the emphasis is usually on forgiveness and the need to submit and live a Spirit-led life that trusts and obeys. Discipleship training that lacks a clear view of preparation for eternity has little more than a "buck up and do good for Jesus" feel to it. The fact that we already belong to heaven and that our lives on earth are a pilgrimage toward heaven is rarely, if ever, taught. Yet that is what adds weight, meaning, and motivation to the process of sanctification. It is the reason Scripture calls us to "set [our] minds on things above" (Col. 3:2).

It is precisely because their hearts were focused on heaven—as Screwtape observes, "rooted in eternity"—that the early church effectively prompted a redemptive revolution so powerful that it formed and framed the entire Western culture for nineteen centuries. Because they were keenly aware that heaven was their home, Christians were willing to suffer, share, and love without thought of return. They were faithful to God without earthly reward, unconcerned with possessions, willing to die—to be brutally martyred—and able to express without intimidation a confidence and courage that the threats of a fleeting, already condemned world could not quell. It is Vibia Perpetua's legacy. It must be ours as well.

Conyers masterfully captures the power of a church rooted in eternity:

> As long as people were taught the idea . . . that our true home is elsewhere, there was a certain satisfaction in the answer itself.

For centuries, the idea that this world is not, by itself, our home —emotionally, spiritually, or even socially—was a compelling idea because it was enormously convincing. It unlocked a secret about human existence that seemed to fit what everyone already sensed about human suffering, human aspirations, and the desire to express life in self-giving love. Neither the flame of persecution nor the ever-present danger of disease or war could extinguish this new lease on life.

Conyers goes on to affirm, "Poverty was still painful but not hopeless. Illness might end in death, but death was not the absolute end. Life took on a creative and vibrant energy because it was harnessed to an overall purpose."[5]

Yet our generation, while admitting that heaven is real, has ceased to embrace its relevance and is paying dearly for the loss. A great divide between here and there, between now and then, has persuaded us that what is heavenly is no earthly good and what is earthly is irrelevant to heaven.

Nothing could be further from the truth.

It is as though God has bought for us at great expense the field of eternity but we have been unwilling to plow, sow, and root ourselves in it.

So what would it take for us to root our hearts in heaven, and how will we know when heaven has indeed become a habit of our hearts? How can we transition admitting that heaven is real to the way we live? How can we once again intimidate the forces of hell by becoming a terrible army with banners rooted in eternity?

Paradise Lost, John Milton's epic poem of God's creation and man's rebellion, concludes with the banishment of Adam and Eve from the Garden of Eden. When Milton finished the manuscript, he gave it to his friend Thomas Ellwood to read. Ellwood returned the work to Milton and remarked, "Thou hast said much here of Paradise Lost, but what hast thou to say of Paradise Found?"[6]

We live in Milton's dilemma. The results of Paradise Lost, the suffering, pain, disappointment, and despair, preoccupy our attention, overshadowing the reality of our scheduled appearance in Paradise reclaimed for us through redemption. This thought forced Milton to write a second work entitled *Paradise Re-*

gained, which captures the compelling *hope* of ultimate resolution of sin and fallenness and the restoration of redeemed mankind to the fullness of God's intended pleasure.

American business in the early 1990s embraced a concept called re-engineering. Reforming the structure and process of industry to guarantee a more effective and efficient flow of work toward a quality product dominated the management advice. According to the management gurus, in the current global marketplace, this would be the only way U.S. firms could maintain their positions in an increasingly competitive environment. While industry is re-engineering, the church needs to re-engineer its focus on eternity to produce more effective workers in an increasingly hostile and competitive spiritual environment.

WE CERTAINLY HOPE SO . . .

This redirecting of our focus from earth toward heaven is best summed up in one word that Scripture uses when it speaks of making heaven our point of reference: *hope.*

Significantly, the Bible offers a concept of hope that goes beyond our normal English usage. In the twentieth century, we understand the word *hope* to be something desired based on a certain level of expectation. *Webster's New World Dictionary of the American Language* states that hope is "a feeling that what is wanted will happen; desire accompanied by expectation." This definition and the popular usage of hope, however, does not require that the expectation be grounded in reality.

For instance, living in Chicago I might say "I hope that the Cubs win the World Series." Quite frankly, there's not a chance! Nevertheless I can use the word *hope* in that context. I might say that I hope the weather will be nice on vacation. Hope does not need to be grounded in reality. It can function as an expression of what we wish for, even if that is simply a "desire accompanied by expectation."

On the other hand, biblical hope is always grounded in realities. It is grounded in a God who is true and whose promises are sure. When we hope in the world to come—in a heaven beyond—we place our hope in a reality that has already been confirmed. Jesus Christ spent forty days here in His other-world form and then disappeared into the world to come. Angels from that world announced that though He had gone to heaven, He would return for us and take us there.

Hope in eternity is founded in the reality of an empty tomb—in the supernatural revelations to the apostle John that unfold for us in the book of Revelation. It is grounded in an understanding that the God who began the process of redemption would hardly, after paying such a high price, fail to bring redemption to consummation and completion. Built upon an assured future reality that we claim by faith, biblical hope is the forward-looking focus of our lives. In fact, as Heb. 11:1 says, faith gives substance to that for which we hope. In effect, we place our hope in a certain future event so compelling that it preoccupies our entire perception of life and, as such, radically alters our behavior in the process.

The difference between our modern use of the word *hope* and the biblical meaning of hope can be reflected in the way a young girl responds after she has been to her first wedding. My guess is that it occurs to her that she would like to have a wedding someday herself. And it's not necessarily related that she's looking forward to getting a husband. More probably she begins envisioning the event itself. She dreams of her dress, the flowers, the bridesmaids, the church, the words spoken, and the whole ambience that surrounds a wedding. In earlier days girls hoping to become brides used to keep things for that day in a box called their *hope* chest. As a girl grows older, her hope grows, too.

All of this hope is not based on a future certainty but is simply a dream in her heart. As such her life is business as usual, and though she periodically wonders, wishes, and hopes for marriage, not much in her life is changed.

Then one day, on a white stallion galloping across the horizon of her life, comes her knight in shining armor. As he approaches, he swoops down, grabs her around the waist, and sweeps her up into his arms. They look lovingly into each other's eyes as he slips the rock on her finger and whispers "June Fourth" in her ear.

Now everything is dramatically changed. So all-consuming is the certain prospect of marriage that it radically alters everything in her life. She views every dress store and bridal magazine through a new lens—a lens formed by the future reality of that day. Her friends are now objects of her invitation list and potential candidates for her wedding party. The certainty and reality of the promise create within her a hope that not only preoccupies her attention but radically alters everything in her life.

That is biblical hope.

A STIRRING HOPE

It is this kind of vibrant hope that stirs every believer—the certain hope of Christ's return and our final, fulfilling home in heaven. As Paul notes in Romans 8, "For in hope we have been saved, but hope that is seen is not hope; for why does one also hope for what he sees? But if we hope for what we do not see, with perseverance we wait eagerly for it" (verses 24–25). Applying hope to the unseen reality of heaven creates within us, as Paul noted, an eager anticipation that is not dimmed or diminished, but rather perseveres through even the most difficult moments in life. In fact, the word that is used in this text for *perseverance* is a Greek word made up of two separate words: *upō* and *menō*. *Upō* means "under," and *menō* means "remain." It is a graphic illustration of the kind of perseverance that hope's eager anticipation kindles in our hearts. No matter what kind of pressure we are under, we remain firm because our hope is fixed on heaven.

In speaking of this hope, Peter breaks out in ecstatic praise as he declares, "Blessed be the God and Father of our Lord Jesus Christ, who according to His great mercy has caused us to be born again to a living hope through the resurrection of Jesus Christ from the dead, to obtain an inheritance which is imperishable and undefiled and will not fade away, reserved in heaven for you, who are protected by the power of God through faith for a salvation ready to be revealed in the last time" (1 Peter 1:3–5).

Note that Peter recognizes that our hope in heaven is not a static, stodgy, cognitive assent within creedal orthodoxy, but rather that it is a *lively* hope. A hope that causes us, as he notes in the following verse, to rejoice greatly "even though now for a little while, if necessary, you have been distressed by various trials." This enlivened prospect in our hearts gives us assurance about our future beyond the difficulties of this life, that even though things get tough on this side, there is a sense of rejoicing in the midst of trials because of what waits for us on the other side. This is not unlike the perspective of Jesus Christ who was even willing to suffer the agony of the cross for the "joy set before Him" (Heb. 12:2).

The biblical word *hope* comes from the Greek root that means *trust.* Thus, our hope in heaven, beyond being based in reality, is about trusting God to keep His Word. This is not a "blind trust." God's Word calls the Holy Spirit the seal, or guarantee, that He will complete the work of redemption and welcome us home for eternity (Eph. 1:13). Every time we sense the promptings of the indwelling Spirit or experience the reality of His presence within us, we have a reminder of God's guarantee that we will make it all the way home.

It's no wonder that Christ could confidently say to His traumatized disciples, "Let not your heart be troubled; believe in God, believe also in Me. . . . I go to prepare a place for you. And if I go and prepare a place for you, I will come again, and receive you to Myself; that where I am, there you may be also" (John 14:1–3).

THE FULLNESS OF HOPE

In its biblical sense, then, hope leans our attention toward the day when heaven will be ours and we will really be there. This forward thrust is not only a transforming ingredient to our Christianity, but it's also therapy to our souls. A life with nothing to look forward to is a life of emptiness and despair. It is hope for something beyond this moment, for something beyond ourselves, that drives the passions of the human soul. When all we have is the moment, we end up saying to ourselves, "There's got to be more to life than this." And when all we have is ourselves and nothing beyond us to promise greater fulfillment, then we feel an encroaching sense of emptiness, insecurity, and disappointment. Hope is our link to a greater beyond, a bigger, better world. Hope is the cord that keeps pulling us upward and onward in life.

We were born to hope. The inner drive to hook our hearts to something beyond the moment, beyond ourselves, is the yearning of heaven in our souls. If, however, hope hinges upon earth-side realities, we find that when we realize what is hoped for, it quickly becomes a memory and is often not nearly as exhilarating as we had hoped. In fact, the anticipation of an event is often more exhilarating than the experience itself, which then sends hope searching again for something new.

HOOKING HOPE ON HIM

Anchoring our hope in our transcendent God and His glorious and certain future expands the best experiences of life. Last night Martie and I drove to the countryside where the amber glow of Chicago's sulfur lights don't mask the glory of God reflected in the universe. There wasn't a cloud in the sky. As we gazed into a tapestry of stars, my heart was drawn to the Maker of it all. As I was struck by the magnitude of the universe, I was reminded of the magnificence of my Creator. The reality that these stars are *here* because He is *there* drew my heart beyond the stars, beyond His creative power, to my relationship with Him—beyond this fleeting moment of my existence to the time when I will see Him face to face and in His presence for eternity sit at His feet as He unfolds the mysteries and miracles of both the macro and the micro elements of His marvelous, wise, and intricate design.

Eventually my gaze dropped toward earth again. As we walked the path that stretched before us, I began to long and hope for something beyond this moment. Something beyond myself—a sense of anticipation and joy, and a flame that only hope in God and heaven can ignite.

Perhaps that is why Dante, in his work *The Inferno*, imagined the words written over the gate entrance into hell, "Leave every hope behind, ye who enter."

It is only when we have attached our hope to the other side that our lives take on meaning on this side, enabling the best of life here to be fully enjoyed. And when life's best moments are over, our hearts still look forward to the wonderful reality that something better is still to come.

Our hope in heaven is grounded in God Himself—unthreatened, unintimidated, and irrevocable. As Paul stated so powerfully,

Who shall separate us from the love of Christ? Shall tribulation, or distress, or persecution, or famine, or nakedness, or peril, or sword? . . . In all these things we overwhelmingly conquer through Him who loved us. For I am convinced that neither death, nor life, nor angels, nor principalities, nor things present, nor things to come, nor powers, nor height, nor depth, nor any other created thing, shall be able to separate us from the love of God, which is in Christ Jesus our Lord. (Rom. 8:35–39)

LESSER HOPES

Our fault is not that we don't hope but rather that our hearts have been content to hope in lesser things. Not necessarily bad or evil things . . . just lesser things. And it's not that we should not have earth-side pursuits. Paul "hoped" to send Timothy to Philippi (Phil. 2:19, 23) and to visit Timothy (1 Tim. 3:14). It's just that our primary hope must be heaven and all that it promises. If that is not the case, our lesser hopes become the driving force of our lives, leaving us shallow, distracted, and often disappointed. When we fix our hope on the other side it defines and often revises our lesser hopes and fills them with meaning and understanding. And when earth-side hopes don't materialize or our dreams turn to nightmares, we can say that "we are struck down, but not destroyed" (2 Cor. 4:9).

At the funeral of former president Richard Milhous Nixon, the Rev. Billy Graham closed his message with an intriguing story from the life of Winston Churchill. The British Prime Minister, as he was making plans for his funeral, asked to be laid in state in the heart of London, in that great architectural masterpiece of Sir Christopher Wren, St. Paul's Cathedral. He requested that his casket be placed under the massive dome in the center of the cathedral. Churchill then requested that two trumpeters be stationed on each side of the balcony that circles the dome. It was his wish that at the close of the service the trumpeter on one side would play taps. When he was finished the trumpeter on the other side was to play reveille.

Christians who are preoccupied with paradise live in the constant hope of hearing reveille, God's wake-up call, when we will be welcomed home by Him.

CHAPTER SIX

WHY HEAVEN SEEMS SO DIM

WHAT HAPPENED TO THE LIGHT AT THE END OF THE TUNNEL?

M y first spiritual impulse related to heaven.

I can still remember sitting in a New Year's Eve service at First Baptist Church in Hackensack, New Jersey. I was six and my dad was preaching about the Second Coming. He remarked, "This could be the year that Christ will come to take us home." I wondered, *If that were to happen, would I be included?* Quite frankly, it was not so much that heaven seemed appealing; it was that I was afraid my parents and sisters would go there (well, actually, I wasn't too sure about my sisters) and that I would be left behind. Nor was the compulsion of my heart the fear of hell. I just wanted to know that if Christ came and took my family, I'd go where my family was going. If that was heaven, I wanted to be there.

God in His grace used those longings to draw my heart to Him. When my dad came home from church he found his pajama-clad son waiting to ask him how to be included in this wonderful invitation of God. My father explained the problem of sin (I knew that there was no sense in trying to fool him about whether I was a sinner or not), opened God's Word, took me by the hand, and introduced me to the Savior. That night this boy became heavenbound.

I have to admit, however, that through the years I've grown accustomed to the privileges of that destination. Like you, I have found it easy to become consumed by the business of life, by earthbound fears and pleasures. And like you, I'm constantly challenged to keep heaven as the ultimate point of reference of who I am and what I do. My fears, frustrations, and insecurities are too easily treated as though this world were all I had. How quickly I forget that my Father is real right now, living in a real place called heaven and sitting on His sovereign throne with His Son. And He gives grace, perspective, mercy, and help in a time of need and the confident hope of a better world in days to come.

Only recently have I once again found my heart turned toward heaven; toward the fact that I was not only built for heaven but redeemed for heaven as well. I have been impressed afresh with the truth that all of life here is but a preparation for, a pilgrimage toward, and an investment in heaven.

I am enjoying the process of coming full circle, back to the time when I was six, where I fixed my heart on heaven as the all-consuming desire and destiny of my life.

WHO WANTS HEAVEN?

Many of us did not have heaven as the first impulse of our homeward journey. Some of us were prompted by the fear of hell. Some of us knew our need for a Savior because our lives had been so wretchedly destroyed by sin. In a sense, salvation for us was a last resort, and if Christ couldn't help us, no one could. In fact, we were hoping not so much for heaven but that He could redesign for us a measure of heaven on earth. Some of us were prompted because life was empty and He promised to fill us, because we knew friends who seemed more satisfied and we wanted to sense the fullness that they had found in Christ. Or it may have been that we were honest seekers. We wondered if there were reasons beyond what we had been told about life and existence. And we wondered if the marvel of the creation didn't have a designer after all, and if it did, that we should take that into account in case someday we had to face Him.

There are dozens of reasons why we are drawn to Christ as Savior. My guess is that very few of us were drawn to Christ purely because we realized that there was heaven to be gained, where Christ and the Father would reign and relate to us and thus fill the longings of our hearts.

Regardless of what prompted us toward a redemptive relationship with Christ, the work of Christ in our lives is ultimately about heaven. Heaven is where the work of redemption finally becomes complete. If I were to ask if you were fully redeemed, you would no doubt think that it was either a trick question or something too theologically deep. Those who answer yes, we are fully redeemed, are correct. Those who answer no, we are not yet fully redeemed, are also correct. We are fully redeemed in that the work was finished on the Cross, and there is nothing more that Christ needs to do or that we can do. Yet we have not yet experienced the fullness of our redemption. We still carry the weight of sin. A common cold or a bout with the flu reminds us that the effects of our fallenness are still with us. We will still taste of death and sorrow. But in the world to come redemption will be fully realized.

Heaven is where we are completely released from every consequence of the Fall and where we are finally restored to an eternal, unhindered relationship with our God. Heaven is the point of Christ's work for us, and He intends it to be the consuming focus of our lives.

AN ETERNAL ECLIPSE

Conyers likens the loss of heaven as our point of reference to an eclipse. He notes that as the eclipse begins there is a dimming of everything; an eerie glow fills the atmosphere and everything on the ground appears duller. He concludes that when heaven is eclipsed by lesser things—things of far less value, like the moon eclipsing the sun—there is a dimming of all that is in our world. Conyers's analogy is an appropriate picture for those of us who give assent to the existence of heaven. Since Satan cannot get us to deny the reality of heaven—it is too much a part of all that we believe—he seeks to block its impact, to diminish its sense of relevance; to eclipse it with things that may be good in their own right (like the moon is a valuable commodity when it reflects the sun).

But the moon was not intended to block the sun. Nor is life intended to dim heaven but rather to reflect its glory. When heaven is dimmed, all we have is this dull, fallen, fleeting planet.

THE DIMMING OF HEAVEN

There are at least six ways in which we become vulnerable to dimming heaven.

The Dreams of Youth

Sometimes we dim heaven innocently through *the dreams of our youth*. When I was engaged to be married, I remember thinking about Christ coming to take me to heaven before my wedding day. I was torn by ambivalent feelings, since I knew I should want heaven more than anything else. But when I met Martie and fell deeply in love with her, it seemed to me that it would be a shame to have wasted all that courtship by not knowing the privilege of being her husband. Quite frankly, I was glad the Lord delayed His coming long enough for us to be married. Then there was the birth of our children and the list of other dreams in those early days that tended to eclipse the wonder and anticipation of heaven in my heart.

Actually, I think that God understands. But had Martie and I been mature and wise enough in those early days of our youth to realize that the anticipated joy of fulfilling our dreams could not compare with the joys of heaven, we would have chosen heaven.

In fact, now that many of my dreams have been realized and I've experienced much of what is good in life, I find that my heart turns more readily toward home. I have found that while life has often been fulfilling, it has not fulfilled my deepest longings and needs. The longer I live, the deeper and greater my anticipation for heaven becomes. While our dreams for the future are normal and even God-given, when they eclipse eternity they work against us.

Distorted Perception About Our Future Home

Second, the brilliance of heaven can be dulled by a *distorted perception of our future home.* Thoughts that an eternity in heaven entails sitting on clouds, playing a harp, singing in a choir, wearing halos, and sporting wings are all less-than-compelling images about heaven.

Mark Twain, who never thought well of either God or heaven, writes in "Captain Stormfield's Visit to Heaven":

> Inside of fifteen minutes I was a mile on my way towards the cloud-banks and about a million people along with me. Most of us tried to fly, but some got crippled and nobody made a success of it.
>
> ... We begun to meet swarms of folks who were coming back. Some had harps and nothing else; some had hymn-books and nothing else; some had nothing at all; all of them looked meek and uncomfortable; one young fellow hadn't anything left but his halo, and he was carrying that in his hand; all of a sudden he offered it to me and says—
>
> "Will you hold it for me a minute?"
>
> Then he disappeared in the crowd.
>
> ... When I found myself perched on a cloud, with a million other people, I never felt so good in my life. . . . I gave my palm branch a wave or two, for luck, and then I tautened up my harp strings and struck in. . . . After about sixteen or seventeen hours, during which I played and sung a little, now and then—always the same tune, because I didn't know any other—I laid down my harp and begun to fan myself with my palm branch.[1]

In heaven Captain Stormfield meets an old friend named Sam Bartlett and asks him, "Now tell me—is this to go on forever? Ain't there anything else for a change?"[2]

One would look in vain to find descriptions such as these in Scripture. Although we will worship God, we will not be like angels in heaven. And while our worship will be a fulfilling expression of our gratitude toward God and, as such, bring us deep satisfaction and spiritual and emotional reward, there is no indication that this worship will be framed in organized choir rehearsals.

Peter Kreeft insightfully notes that we have lost the sense of the powerful, moving, biblical imagery of heaven—a throne filled with the awesome glory of God and awestruck worshipers who spontaneously revel in His presence. We don't imagine masses of powerful, magnificent angels who guarantee and actualize the sovereign plans of the God of history, a place filled with saints and martyrs and the faithful of all the ages who finally know what bliss is. And all of this wrapped with celestial blasts of trumpets and massive voices singing praise to God and celebrating His gracious gift of redemption. We have traded the magnificent for weak, anemic images of cherubs and an ethereal nothingness in the sky. "More modern, more up-to-date substitutes—Heaven as a comfortable feeling of peace and kindness, sweetness and light, and God as a vague grandfatherly benevolence, a senile philanthropist—are even more insipid."[3]

Perhaps it's easy to create distorted images of heaven since few descriptions of heaven exist in Scripture. While we read that there will be streets of gold and gates of pearl, during the course of eternity we'll probably get used to those. And in comparison to the blazing glory of the presence of God they will no doubt pale into insignificance. We know from Scripture that Christ is preparing a place for us. We know that God will be present and that we will delight in Him with unhindered joy and satisfaction. But we don't know much beyond these details. Someone has suggested that perhaps God didn't tell us much about heaven because if we knew how exhilarating it would be, we'd be jumping off skyscrapers to get there.

God wants us to appreciate and enjoy this earth until He calls us home. By comparison, though, the best of what we have here cannot be measured with what we will have there. Interesting, isn't it, that this fallen place is filled with dramatic, awe-inspiring, seemingly unspoiled areas for us to enjoy—the Caribbean islands, a Florida beach, the rocky coasts of California, the sun-drenched Hawaiian islands, the English countryside, or the marvel of bustling Paris or New York. And this world offers many pleasures—an evening of fine dining, the camaraderie of a few good friends, the companionship of a faithful dog. Yet all of these earth-side experiences are under the damage of the Fall.

By comparison, imagine what the new heavens, the new earth, and the New Jerusalem will be like, undamaged and undefiled by sin. Imagine the best of what we have here. Think about what makes your day or what would exhilarate and fill your senses to the maximum. And then think of the fact that heaven is far better.

"Far better" is Scripture's most profound description of our eternal home. When Paul said in Philippians chapter one that he had a desire to depart and be with Christ, for that is better by far (Phil. 1:23), he was stating that, comparatively speaking, heaven is beyond our best experiences here on earth. And when you think of it, even our best experiences here lack something in terms of what we had expected, and they are also too soon ended.

Martie and I have a couple of special places that we love to get away to, and we laugh about the fact that sometimes even before we go we begin to feel a twinge of sadness that soon our time there will be done and we'll have to return to our routine. Think about what it would be like to experience all that is far better . . . forever.

Satan is a master at taking what is true, permitting us to cling to it as a statement of creed, and then distorting our perception of it and in the process robbing it of its impact and its transforming influence on our lives. Kreeft observes:

> Our pictures of Heaven simply do not move us. . . . It is . . . our pictures of Heaven and of God that threatens faith most potently today. Our pictures of Heaven are dull, platitudinous and syrupy; therefore, so is our faith, our hope, and our love of Heaven.
>
> It is surely a Satanic triumph of the first order to have taken the fascination out of a doctrine that must be either a fascinating lie or a fascinating fact. . . . If it's dull, it doesn't matter whether it's a dull lie or a dull truth. Dullness, not doubt, is the strongest enemy of faith . . ."[4]

Do we really think that God, who built us for an unhindered relationship with Him, who longed—and acted through the death of His Son—to restore us to that ultimate level of satisfaction, would plan for us an eternity of boredom?

I doubt it!

The Intrigues of Our Lives

Third, *the intrigues of our lives* tend to dim heaven's hold on our hearts. Hundreds of earth-side concerns threaten to consume our emotions and distract our attention, creating perhaps good but lesser priorities for us to pursue. Whether it be our careers, our families, our friendships, or our frustrations, there is much that will compete with our focus on heaven.

Clearly, God intended that these interests occupy our minds and hearts so that we would responsibly fulfill our duties to them. But He never intended that they would supplant heaven in our hearts. He intended rather that our careers would be a springboard to eternal gain; that our families would be drawn to heaven by our examples as parents and spouses; that our friends would see in our lives the glory of a risen Christ and the reality of a Father who is in heaven; and that our enemies would know the forgiveness that opens heaven's door by the extension of our compassion and redemptive actions toward them.

God has not called us to be so consumed with heaven that we cocoon ourselves in anxious anticipation of getting there. But He has planned that all of our temporal targets be viewed in line with the transcending reality of the world to come.

The Lure of the Tangible

Fourth, we are prone to be seduced away from an affectionate attachment to heaven by our tendency to favor that which is *rational and material.* Heaven is an intrinsically supernatural place. It has no parallel on this planet. Yet, because our scientific age accepts only that which can be proven in scientific laboratories or academic halls, many people, including Christians, have come to value only that which is verifiable. Transcendent realities like heaven quickly become irrelevant and are viewed as the foolish fantasies of weak, superstitious people who cannot cope with life on earth as it is.

Even those of us who don't understand the philosophical basis for materialism still find ourselves absorbed by materialism. We give high priority to having things and stockpiling earth-bound treasures. While God has indeed given us all good things to enjoy, He never intended the things in our environment to eclipse our longing for heaven. In fact, the lesson we fail to learn is that even when we become absorbed with material gain we still have longings that this present world is unable to satisfy.

Religious Temporalism

The fifth factor that dims heaven in our hearts is even more subtle. It is what I call *religious temporalism*—having spiritual goals based on temporal rather than eternal standards. Unfortunately, spiritual leaders often become entangled in the perception that the kingdom of God consists of building plans, budget size, body counts, and a whole list of other earth-side statistics.

It's fascinating to note that the New Testament church never viewed their success in terms of numbers. Their success was measured in their ability to overcome the world, to live the values of heaven, and to enlist recruits to join them in their pilgrim procession.

The apostles gave little attention to the size and numbers of the early church. Instead, all the recognition went to the God of heaven and the Christ of glory. The early believers measured their success in this world in terms of eternal gain.

The most dangerous lie of religious temporalism is the teaching that with enough faith you can find the fulfillment of wealth, health, and happiness here on earth. There is not a strand of truth in this heretical teaching. In fact, those who have been most transformed by the reality of heaven have often suffered the loss of happiness or health, and at times they have been impoverished because of their faith. God promises us heaven there and then, not here and now. As we shall learn, this fallen world is not a friend to grace. Christ clearly predicted that in this world we would have trouble (John 16:33).

It is interesting to note that when Christ came, the disciples were frightfully naive about heaven. One might assume that having been schooled in Judaism they would have a keen understanding of the world to come. Yet their thoughts of a future paradise focused on the dream that a Messiah would come and overthrow the Roman occupation, establish His rule on earth, and restore Israel to its former glory. It was not heaven there, but heaven *here* on earth that they anticipated.

In fact, the whole religious environment of Christ's day had minimalized the thought of heaven. Of the Sadducees it is noted, " . . . not only would the Sadducees have a prosperous material life—thus making a blessed afterlife superfluous—but they could also fully experience the presence of God here on earth."[5] In fact, the Sadducees held that there is no afterlife. Both their theology and their affluence made it unnecessary. The Pharisees, on the other hand, affirmed the reality of a life to come, yet, as McDannell and Lang observed: "We can only speculate about how the Pharisees viewed the possibility of life after death. Since they were primarily concerned with the ritual dimension of Judaism, only fleeting indications of their beliefs can be found in ancient sources."[6]

Given these prevailing religious attitudes, it's no wonder that the disciples' view of heaven was indeed dim. Their lack of focus on heaven was buttressed by their environment, both physical and religious.

We also suffer from similar influences. Our affluence and relative comfort make heaven less compelling. Our obsession with earth-side rules, codes, programs, and participation in religious activities blurs our long-term vision. We are often consumed by the busyness of our Christianity.

Heaven has not always been so dim. And it is significant to note that when it was brighter, the world felt its impact.

In medieval times the whole thought of heaven and the afterlife was a compelling force in all of society. Heaven consistently made its mark in the writings of philosophers, in the great music, in fine art. But since that time, and in particular through the Age of Enlightenment and into the nineteenth and twentieth centuries, there has been a steady erosion of the theological, philosophical, and scientific support for a strong belief in the afterlife.

The Skepticism of Society

This eroding belief has given rise to the sixth reason for the dimming of heaven's reality in our hearts: *the skepticism of society.* We live in *a culture that denies heaven as a compelling reality.*

Though the philosophers Descartes and Kant both believed in the afterlife, they spent much time in their writings debating and discounting the more detailed accounts of what the afterlife would be like, stating that human senses and reason had no capacity to grasp life beyond the grave. The reality of heaven continued under attack in the influential writings of the founding father of Protestant liberalism, Friedrich Schleiermacher. Though he did not publicly deny the existence of heaven, Schleiermacher continued Kant's legacy of skepticism about the afterlife.

In the secular realm, philosophers like Hume, Hegel, and Feuerbach dismissed altogether hope for life after death, as did Russian theorists Marx and Lenin and the founder of psychoanalysis, Sigmund Freud. Numerous scientists, including Charles Darwin with his theory of evolution, argued against both the existence of God and immortality.

Kreeft chronicles the demise of heaven as our primary reference point. Through medieval times, "earth was Heaven's womb, Heaven's nursery, Heaven's dress rehearsal." He writes, "Heaven was the meaning of the earth." Now in the late twentieth century he notes that the "glory has departed"—that we no longer "live habitually in this medieval mental landscape." He concludes:

> If we are typically modern, we are bored, jaded, cynical, flat, and burnt out. . . . If we were not so bored and empty, we would not have to stimulate ourselves with increasing dosages of sex and violence—or just constant busyness. Here we are in the most fantastic fun and games factory ever invented—modern technological society—and we are bored, like a spoiled rich kid in a mansion surrounded by a thousand expensive toys. Medieval people by comparison were like peasants in toyless hovels—and they were fascinated. Occasions for awe and wonder seemed to abound: birth and death and love and light and darkness and wind and sea and fire and sunrise and star and tree and bird and human mind—and God and Heaven. But all these things have not changed, we have. The universe has not become empty and we, full; it has remained full and we have become empty, insensitive to its fullness, cold hearted.[7]

Our society is a by-product of these materialistic, rationalistic notions, and since there is no encouragement for us to accept heaven as a natural continuation of our existence, it is no wonder that our hearts struggle to keep our attention fixed on the world to come. As the German theologian Karl Rahner laments, "Belief in eternal life has grown weaker in the consciousness of modern people." Lamenting the erosion of this in even the church, he notes, "There are Christians who are sure of the existence of God . . . but who do not think it necessary to show any great interest in the question of eternal life."[8] A sharp sense of heaven as a literal point of reference has been further eroded by the highly influential writings and teachings of more modern theologians such as Neibuhr, Tillich, and Bultmann, who refused to affirm a literal afterlife in a literal place called heaven. Instead, they considered the biblical teachings about life beyond the grave as symbolic, and in some cases mythologic.

This has left much of mainstream Christianity in the Western world void of a compelling hope in heaven, lacking a passion for the world beyond the grave. For those beliefs they bear the ridicule of both the philosophical, scientific, and religious world. They are viewed as the residual elements of a superstitious, narrow, nonintellectual, medieval mind-set.

As we have moved from the Age of Enlightenment through modernism and to what is now called the "post-modern era," there has been an interesting revitalization of curiosity about the afterlife. Post-modern thinking is marked by a diminished interest in classical reason and logic. History cannot be trusted, given the prejudicial perspectives of those who wrote it. If reason, logic, and history are no longer points of reference for our understanding of the world around us, then we are free to think any way we want about anything in the past, present, or future. Intrinsic instincts for something out there beyond this life captivates our thoughts. However, thoughts of an afterlife do not include a biblical future where there is a hell to be shunned and a heaven to be gained. Rather, Eastern thoughts of reincarnation or some kind of mystical floating nirvana where all is joy and peace have captured the modern mind.

Of all the false philosophies now prevalent in American society, none promotes a relationship with the real God of the universe who will judge the living and the dead and grant those who have embraced His redemption a literal eternity with Him. It is as though modern culture has determined what people were created to experience and then designed it after their own notions.

Whether Shirley MacLaine is writing about life after life after life through reincarnation, or Betty Eadie is writing of having a God coming within as she—and any willing reader—is "embraced by the light," best-selling books try to redesign eternity after personal whims. Readers can choose whatever they wish to believe, and they can dismiss whatever they do not like, including the idea of sin, a holy and just God who must judge sin, and the possibility of a personal relationship with God.

But the Bible makes very clear that God is personal and heaven is real. And though we know only a few things about our future home, what we do know gives us great hope—a hope that adjusts our focus and refuses to allow lesser influences to dim the brilliance of eternity.

What would it take then to reignite the reality of heaven in our hearts?

CHAPTER SEVEN

REIGNITING THE REALITY

HEAVEN IN OUR OWN HISTORY

After defecting to the United States, Orestes Lorenzo Perez knew he had to rescue his family from Cuba. So one Saturday afternoon, flying low in a borrowed Cessna to avoid radar, he swooped down into Cuba, past his former neighborhood, and landed in traffic on a coastal road. His family ran to the plane, and they were soon leaving the Cuban shore, en route to freedom.

His wife, Victoria, had waited patiently. But it was hard. Going to America seemed to her like going to heaven. "When I saw the plane, I screamed to my children, 'That's your father!'"

"I grabbed both of them and we ran," she said. As they ran, one of the kids lost a shoe. "Forget the shoe!" Victoria screamed. "Father is in the plane!"[1]

After two years of separation, the family had been reunited. To Victoria and Orestes, their new home in America is like heaven: a place of freedom, a place where they can realize their dreams.

For Victoria, America had been a vague reality. She knew her husband was there and that it would be better there, but she had few details to make it real in her heart.

For us heaven is often vague. As America was for Victoria, it remains a distant dream. A biblical fantasy land. A religious Disney World in the sky. Refocusing on heaven as our ultimate point of reference requires that we find a way to come to grips with its reality in our hearts.

Visions of heaven abound. Normally they evoke thoughts of clouds, angels, worship, the presence of God, and unlimited joy and peace. For you, it may be a place where all your dreams come true. Or where you sit at the apostle Paul's feet, learning the details of theology. Or you may picture having a powwow with Peter about how emotions are different in heaven, or just spending lots of time asking Old Testament saints, such as Noah, Moses, and David, about how they struggled with their faith during hard times.

While some of our versions of heaven may be somewhat fanciful, Scripture gives us many clues about what heaven will really be like. Knowing what heaven will be like and how we will appear in heaven is important to reigniting its reality.

WHAT ISAIAH, PAUL, AND JOHN SAW

Three devoted followers of God were given intimate portraits of God and His heaven. The prophet Isaiah had a vision of God the Father on the throne (Isaiah 6). Isaiah found God so awesome and full of glory that he cried out, "Woe to me . . . I am ruined! Because I am a man of unclean lips." The apostle Paul was caught up into "the third heaven . . . Paradise, and heard inexpressible words, which a man is not permitted to speak" (2 Cor. 12:1-4).

In the final book of the Bible, the apostle John shares a revelation of not only the end times but of heaven to come. In his sneak preview of heaven, John sees all creatures paying homage to the glorified Christ and the church celebrating a marriage supper with Christ. John concludes with a wondrous description of the beauties of the New Jerusalem (Rev. 22:1-5).

From these descriptions we can be confident that heaven is where God is, where Christ the King receives His proper honor, and where sin cannot exist. You may reflect on these brief glimpses and think, *If I had such an accurate vision of heaven, eternity might affect more fully my life in the present world.* That's probably true. Those three saints had a distinctive edge on us. Of course, so did Christ, who not only came from heaven but returned to heaven. Is it any wonder that so much of His ministry was marked by attempts to stretch our frame of reference beyond the here and now to the reality of the better world beyond?

But God has given us a key that opens the door to a deeper sense of the reality of heaven.

FORTY AMAZING DAYS

Our sense of the reality of eternity is affirmed by recalling one compelling period of time in history: the dramatic season of *heaven on earth* during the appearances of Christ after His resurrection and before His subsequent return to heaven. Christ stayed on earth for forty days (Acts 1:3) in His heaven-fit, resurrected body. The presence of His eternal form re-engineered for eternity provides irrefutable proof of the reality of the world to come. It should fuel our faith in these closing days of the twentieth century.

When we reread the Scriptures that describe the post-resurrection Christ, we find much to cheer us about heaven and our future there. We see Christ in His eternal, re-engineered form in the garden with Mary. He walked with two disciples on the road to Emmaus. He joined a gathering of disciples in a closed room. Eight days later He issued a dramatic invitation for Thomas to touch His wounds and confirm that He was indeed the Christ. Though His body was again whole, the marks of His crucifixion suffering were still visible.

Later, Jesus appeared in His other-world form at the Sea of Galilee and instructed Peter and the disciples, who had caught no fish, to cast their net over the right side of the boat. They caught more than their net could bear.

HIS REAL, RESURRECTED BODY

In each of these appearances Christ appeared markedly different, yet He was recognizable as the same Christ whom they had known and loved for three years.

We celebrate the incarnation of Christ and His sacrifice on the cross for our sins. Yet, we give far less attention to His return to earth in His eternal form after He had finished the work of His incarnation. But that forty-day visit—accomplished in a new, yet real, body—displays the reality of the world to come.

Jesus demonstrated an important truth: Redemption is not complete at the Cross or even in His resurrection, but it will be fully realized when we join Him on the other side.

Jesus' reappearance in His heavenly body demonstrated that heaven is a real place. In a dramatic moment in the sight of His stunned disciples, Christ ascended to heaven. The angels appeared and promised that He would return to take His followers there as well. Luke reported in Acts 1:11 that these angels from heaven said, "Men of Galilee, why do you stand looking into the sky? This Jesus, who has been taken from you into heaven, will come in just the same way as you have watched Him go into heaven."

At a real time in history angels appeared from heaven to announce that Jesus went to heaven, a *real* place, where He would dwell as a *real* person.

All of this makes for great divine theater. With the world as His stage, God sent His Son back to us again in His other-world form; a real but dramatically different form than this world had ever seen. Then, at the close of this forty-day experience with the reality of the world to come, Christ ascended from their midst and two angels appeared to assure His followers that this real Person had gone to a real place. The whole world at this point should have risen in thunderous applause for the best-yet special effects, and then as the curtain dropped it would be back to business as usual.

What is interesting, however, is that once they were touched by the revelation of the eternal Christ, they could never return to business as usual. Struck by the reality of the world to come —by the fact that they too would be real persons in a real place with a real Savior once again—all they did from that point on was driven and defined by heaven as their all-consuming point of reference. The fact that the world to come was not only a reality but *really theirs* became their hope, courage, and confidence in a world that mocked, scoffed, mistreated, marginalized, and persecuted them. This revelation gave them a deeper sense of community, love, and involvement. It drove them to reach out to their fellow citizens, who were in need of a Savior and headed toward hell.

REAL PERSONS IN THAT REAL PLACE

What made this divine drama so compelling was that the disciples had been assured that they too would be real people in that real place on the other side of their graves. The New Testament guarantees for us that Christ was the firstborn among many brethren (Rom. 8:29; Col. 1:18; Heb. 1:6), which means that He was the first to be raised with a body fit for the world to come, and that all those who are resurrected to eternal life will receive eternal bodies as well. John assures us that when we see Him we will be like Him for we shall see Him as He is (1 John 3:1–3). Then Paul underscores our other-side existence when he writes that our earthly bodies are like a tent, something temporary taken on a pilgrimage, and our heavenly bodies will be built by God fit for eternity in heaven (2 Cor. 5:1–5). And in the chapter that celebrates the Resurrection, he launches into an extensive essay about the reality of our risen bodies, stating that they will be different yet similar to our earthly bodies, as a plant is different yet similar to the seed that is sown and becomes the plant. In fact, Paul compares our earthly bodies with our heavenly bodies by saying that while the earthly body is perishable, the heavenly body is not perishable; that while it is prone to dishonor, it is raised in glory; sown in weakness, it is raised in power; sown as a natural body, it is raised as a spiritual body (1 Cor. 15:35–44).

Paul concludes 1 Corinthians 15 by declaring that our bodies will be changed "in the twinkling of an eye," and that death will have no dominion over us (verses 50–57).

A PROVEN REALITY

Christ's appearance in His eternal form gives evidence of the reality of our existence in heaven as real people. If you wonder what you will be like in heaven, look at Christ in Acts 1:3–4 and the record of Christ's appearances at the close of the gospels.

Think specifically of all that the real re-engineered Christ was able to do with his "built for heaven" body.

His body was able to be touched. In that closed room with the disciples He invited a skeptical Thomas to touch His wounds, that he himself might verify the reality of the risen Lord. His voice was recognized by Mary in the Garden. What is fascinating to me is that His re-engineered body was trans-material. He was able to appear in a room whose doors and windows were locked tight. (The only other person I've ever known to be trans-material is my mother. She could appear from nowhere in an instant.) Scripture records that He ate with His disciples in His post-resurrected form. Think of eating on the other side: calorie-free chocolate and fat-free sirloin steaks! Actually, although we aren't sure that there will be eating in the new heaven and the new earth, we do know that our eternal bodies will be capable of that function. It may be, as St. Augustine suggested, that while our bodies will have the capacity to eat, they will be released from the need to eat. So we will eat only when we choose to eat or when eating is appropriate to the moment.[2]

The point is not that we will actually be doing all of these activities on a regular basis, but that our resurrected form will be so real that it at least will be capable of these functions. Any thought that we will be cosmic dust floating through an ethereal experience is not biblical. When we get there we will be real people.

Lewis describes the reality of our other-side form by saying,

> It is not the picture of an escape from any and every kind of nature into some unconditional and utterly transcendent life. It is the picture of a new human nature, and a new nature in general, being brought into existence. . . . That is the picture—not of unmaking, but of remaking. The old field of space, time, matter, and the senses is to be weeded, dug, and sown for a new crop. We may be tired of that old field; God is not.[3]

ETERNITY WITHIN

It is intriguing to note that our souls upon their creation became eternal entities. Our resurrected bodies will be the eternal homes of our souls. It is our souls that are marked by personality. They retain memories and bear the uniqueness of our being. It is in our souls that we worship God, dream, and contemplate. It is our souls, housed in different though uniquely similar bodies, that will continue to reflect our personhood.

Heaven, in a very real sense, is a continuation of all that was begun on this side. A continuation of the same soul that is me in a body re-engineered for eternity. Released from the ravages and bondage of sin, we are set free in unfettered liberty to worship and praise the God of heaven and His Son, our Redeemer. Finally, we will experience the unhindered joy, satisfaction, and fulfillment that God intended for us before there was sin, disappointment, and despair.

Recently a friend who is approaching her eighties told me, "My body is a lot slower, but I don't feel older on the inside." I've heard a lot of older people reflect that sentiment. Could it be that their feeling is a reflection of the eternal nature of the soul? Our souls do not grow old but continue in our eternal bodies. A fascinating thought. Eternity is already within us as a pledge of the world to come. It now becomes our privilege to groom our souls for the world to come. In fact, our souls preserve our personal identity and guarantee recognition on the other side.

THE REALITY OF OUR PLACE

Not only will we be real people, but we will be in a real place. Heaven is not a figment of divine imagination, some mystical, floating, ethereal, never-never land. As the angels made clear in Acts 1, it is a real place. And, more importantly, it will be our home forever. I'm wondering if the angels' announcement to the disciples—"This Jesus, who has been taken up from you into heaven, will come in just the same way as you have watched Him go into heaven"—brought to mind Christ's assurance to them just several days before: "In My Father's house are many dwelling places; if it were not so, I would have told you; for I go to prepare a place for you. And if I go and prepare a place for you, I will come again, and receive you to Myself; that where I am, there you may be also" (John 14:2–3).

Embrace the reality. He is now preparing a real place in which we will actually live as real people. As Christ was charged with the creation of the universe and gave it resplendent perfection in both micro and macro design, His creative energy is preparing a personalized residence for me, for you, and all who are redeemed.

REALLY HOME

Igniting the reality of heaven where I will be a real person in a real personalized place living with the reality of my risen Lord and Savior carries with it two profound revelations.

The first is that heaven is truly *home*. This realization gives rise to the second revelation: I am an *alien* and a *pilgrim* here. Saint John the divine said it best, "God is at home; we are in the far country."

Webster's Ninth New Collegiate Dictionary notes that home is where our "domestic affections lie." As we used to say, "Home is where the heart is." That is why a cowboy can sing, "Home, home on the range" and why someone far away from his place of residence can exclaim, "I love this place; I feel so at home here." It is why Christians have sung, "This world is not my home," and why Don Wyrtzen could write the lyrics, "Just think of stepping on shore and finding it heaven! Of touching a hand and finding it God's! Of breathing new air and finding it celestial! Of waking up in glory and finding it home."[4]

We, as heaven-bound pilgrims, are the real homeless ones on this planet. Christ never considered Himself at home here. He knew that He had come from heaven and that He was going back to heaven and that heaven was truly home. This left Him wonderfully unhindered in functioning on behalf of His Father's mission. The disciples had in a sense become homeless as well. They had given up their homes, careers, familiar places, and family to journey with Christ toward an eternal home.

The mission of Christ, as we have already noted, was never intended to culminate at the Cross. The Cross and the empty grave were merely a means to kick the door of heaven open for us so that we could go home to be with Him. Home is where you feel comfortable, secure, safe, and at peace. In a very real sense Jesus Christ had become the disciples' home away from home. As long as they were with Him they felt at home. That is exactly why they were so traumatized when He told them that He was leaving them (John 13, 14).

Christ instructed them on how to live after His departure. But traumatized by His impending departure, they were unable to hear instructions for their lives and ministries without Him. So He interrupted His strategic session on survival without Him to patiently answer the rather testy questions of both Peter and Thomas regarding His departure. It should not go unnoticed that He took great pains at this point to assure them that He was going to His home to make a home for them (John 14:1–6). As long as they would believe this and count heaven to be their home, they would be able to function here unhindered. Christ made it clear that He came here to take us there to be with Him. Heaven is truly our home.

FREE AT LAST

This truth has tremendous ramifications not only on our freedom to function without the hindrances that come when we focus only on our comfort, safety, and security, but it also radically alters our self-perception. We are truly, as Peter stated, aliens and strangers in this land. As Paul noted in Philippians, we are citizens of heaven and, as such, are simply in transit. As citizens we are to proudly display the glory of the land to which we belong and to magnify the name of our King through our attitudes and actions. Our behavior, perspectives, thoughts, and conclusions about life and liberty are dramatically different than this world's. As home-bound citizens of heaven we are from a different culture with different standards and radically different values and ethics.

As home-focused travelers, we seek to draw others to Christ and then compel them to join us in our march toward Zion.

Like the homeless in our cities, we have no attachments to hinder us. We are free to serve Him with nothing to lose *here* and everything to gain *there*. We can lose our houses or jobs, yet we do not sink in despair, because none of these commodities brings lasting safety or peace. When the Spirit taps us for our most precious commodities—our resources, our money, or even our children—we are not destroyed. We can become non-negotiably faithful *here* because home is *there*.

That's the lesson many believers in China learned as they suffered for their faith. The possible loss of earthly goods did not matter, but honoring the Savior did. One church leader, Lin Xiangao, was sentenced to sixteen months in prison and was barely out when he was condemned again. This time the sentence was twenty years of labor in a coal mine in a northern province. His job was to link coal cars as miners filled them. One slip could mean injury or death.

During several "political study" meetings during that imprisonment, officials wanted Lin to denounce other Christians, and they promised him rewards for doing so. He refused. Once they tried to make Pastor Lin denounce Christ. He was unmoved. "Even if you prolong my sentence or kill me, I cannot criticize Christ." Lin remained in prison the full twenty years.

A few years ago writer Fergus Bordewich visited a clandestine church located in a third-floor room—a Chinese underground church in the heart of Canton. Everyone in the attic church knew that the gathering was illegal. Police might burst in at any time to beat them and drag them away. Leading them in worship was Pastor Lin.[5]

Neither Lin nor his church members hesitated to worship God in that place, despite the threat of suffering and jail. Why? Because their hope was fixed on heaven, their future home.

PEOPLE MAKE THE PLACE

It's important to note that when Christ spoke of heaven He didn't describe exotic neighborhoods, square footage, Jacuzzis, or multiple-car garages. He spoke of heaven as the place where He lives and where we will experience the joy of being with Him.

I learned a long time ago that people make the place. My wife has a knack for making our home a pleasant, enjoyable, rewarding environment in which to live. From her color choices to pictures on the wall, she surrounds our family with a sense of warmth and beauty. I love to come home to the environment she has created . . . unless, that is, I come home and she is not there. On those rare occasions, I feel an emptiness that diminishes the delight of coming home. It is true for all of us—no matter how nice our home is: people make the place. Ask the widow, the empty-nester, the spouse whose partner has gone

on an extended business trip, and they will tell you the same
. . . people make the place.

For Victoria and her children, the highlight in their rescue
was a reunion with their husband and father. When the plane
landed Victoria didn't shout, "Let's go to America!"—rather she
exclaimed, "That's your father!"

And it is Christ and our Father who will make our home in
heaven so special.

The fact is that the more intimate our walk and experiences
are with Christ here, the more we will long for heaven and the
sooner it will become the instinctive point of reference for us. In
fact, could it be that heaven seems unreal for us because our
relationship with Christ has become so habitual? So we no longer
desire, as Paul did, to go home and be with Him, which, as Paul
noted, would be far better? (Phil. 1:23).

Do you want to long for heaven? Then cultivate a deepening
relationship with Christ.

If our hearts lean toward Christ who is in heaven, we'll be
drawn there in our thoughts and emotions. But if our hearts are
earthbound, then heaven will be unreal, distant, and dim.

The liberating realization that heaven is home is what caused
G. K. Chesterton to write that for the Christian, optimism is
based on the fact that we are not home in this world. "The modern philosopher had told me again and again that I was in the
right place, and I had still felt depressed even in acquiescence."
But he notes that when he "heard that I was in the wrong place
. . . my soul sang for joy, like a bird in spring." He writes, "I
knew now . . . why I could feel homesick at home."[6]

The reality of heaven as home compelled Malcolm Muggeridge
to observe: "The only ultimate tragedy we can experience on
earth is to feel at home here."

ARE WE HOME YET?

I'm reminded of an elderly missionary couple who arrived at
their home port after years of faithful service. At the dock, an
ambassador and his wife who had returned on the ship with
them were surrounded by a crowd. Roses were bestowed on his
wife as photographers' flashes exploded, and an attentive, ad-

miring press and public hung on every word as he spoke of the joy of serving his government and coming home. As the missionary couple walked unnoticed through that crowd, the wife, with hot tears streaking her face, wondered out loud to her husband, "Why is it that we have given our whole lives to Christ and yet there is no one here to honor us and welcome us home?" Her understanding husband, reaching beyond that lonely moment, said to her, "Honey, we're not home yet."

It is this wonderful refocusing of both our heads and our hearts that enables us to understand Paul's enigmatic statement in Philippians 1 when he exclaimed, "For to me, to live is Christ, and to die is gain" (v. 21). Without the confidence that heaven is a compelling reality and the only reasonable point of reference, we would assume with the world that for me to live is gain and to die is loss.

DYING IS GAIN

Paul's formula is critical to readjusting our point of reference to the reality of eternity. The need for gain is intrinsic in our fallenness. Because of the loss of what we were meant to be, we are incomplete. Sensing the loss, we hunger for gain, for something more. But the problem is not that we hunger for gain, but that we pursue it on this side of eternity, thinking that if somehow we could gain enough and keep what we have gained, then we could be happy, complete, safe, and secure.

Complicating that misplaced passion for gain is the sneaking suspicion that Christ will sabotage our gain on this side. That somehow Christ equates to loss on this earth, even though He has guaranteed the reality of heaven on the other side. We fear that if we take Him seriously and submit to His lordship, He may ask us for our money or maybe call our children away into service in the church—or worse yet overseas to missions. Christ becomes a potential liability when we think that we may have to give up what we have gained in earth-side comfort to be fully devoted to Him. This nagging suspicion that Christ means loss often keeps us from an unflinching commitment to serve Him.

Deep down, we are simply swallowing Satan's lie: "True gain is to be achieved here." True gain, however, is being restored to our created purpose, an unhindered, satisfying experience of a relationship with the God of the universe. As the lover of my soul, He intends heaven as the place where we know final gain and eternal fulfillment.

Missionary Jim Elliot made heaven the centerpoint of his life. "He is no fool who loses what he cannot keep to gain what he cannot lose," he wrote in his journal. This philosophy released him to serve Christ even in the face of death as he bled to death in the Curaray River that winds through the jungles of Ecuador. Though for Jim being fully devoted to Christ here meant loss, it clearly was gain on the ledger sheet of eternity. He was home . . . to die is gain. And not only gain for him, but gain for a tribe that would ultimately come to know Christ as well.

Living for Christ is really not possible until we understand and embrace the fact that dying is gain. And that is not possible until we firmly believe that heaven is real. When we affirm that truth in the depths of our souls, then we are finally free to live for Christ, even if that requires earth-side loss.

Isn't this what Paul had in mind when he deemed all the gain of his life insignificant compared to living for Christ? After he looked at all his supposed accomplishments, he concluded,

> I consider everything a loss compared to the surpassing great-ness of knowing Christ Jesus my Lord, for whose sake I have lost all things. I consider them rubbish, that I may gain Christ and be found in him, not having a righteousness of my own that comes from the law, but that which is through faith in Christ—the righ-teousness that comes from God and is by faith. (Phil. 3:8–9 NIV)

ALL GOOD THINGS TO ENJOY

That is not to say that when God in His grace enables us to enjoy a measure of gain here that we should be inflicted with guilt about it. As Paul told Timothy, "God . . . richly supplies us with all things to enjoy" (1 Tim. 6:17). What it does mean is that we hold our gain loosely, ready to give it up. It means that we count all that we have as a temporary blessing. If Christ requires that we surrender it for His glory and the gain of His kingdom, then we gladly comply. For us the whole point of our living is a personal relationship with Jesus Christ, who guarantees us final and fulfilling gain on the other side.

When we are consumed with the reality of heaven, Christ is free to consume us on earth. When we realize that final gain is there and then, we are free to live for Him here and now. When we put gain in its place, we begin to enjoy Christ in His rightful place—the all-consuming center of our lives.

When heaven is the transcendent target of our living, then we indeed have the best of both worlds: Christ here and gain there. We are assured of Christ's presence and protection here, and ultimately the guarantee of paradise there, where He is the substance of our eternal gain.

This may be why C. S. Lewis profoundly noted in *Mere Christianity*, "Aim at heaven and you'll get earth thrown in. Aim at earth and you'll get neither."[7]

CHAPTER EIGHT

FOR
HEAVEN'S SAKE

REALITY CHECK

I n 1988 a Bible teacher announced in his booklet entitled *Eighty-eight Reasons Why Christ Will Return in '88* that the second coming of Christ would occur that September. The book received much publicity and attracted a large following. His followers became passionate in their belief that Christ would be returning within the year. A video was released that dramatized the detailed proof of the prediction, and people sent me copies of the booklet and video, hoping as president of Moody that I would help warn the church.

I reviewed the booklet and did not believe the author accurately handled Scripture passages, particularly in light of the fact that Christ predicted that no man would know the time of His coming. Of course, September came and went without Christ's return. Among Christians, a few people were greatly disappointed, some were indifferent, and others felt embarrassed by the prophecy.

Still, my reaction—and that of many Christians—was an increased awareness that Christ could come back at any time. The implications sent my mind heavenward.

On the actual September morning that the author had pin-pointed for the return of Christ, I rose from bed and for a mo-ment wondered, *What if I am wrong and he is right? What if this is the day?* At the breakfast table, my family engaged in a lively discussion about it.

My daughter, Libby, walked down the driveway with me, con-tinuing the discussion as I headed for my car to drive to my office. As I stepped into my car, Libby waved and said, "Hey, Dad... see ya in heaven."

My thoughts during that day were often of heaven.

Think of the difference it would make if each day heaven were so real to us that we anticipated being there by the day's end.

ETERNALLY DIFFERENT

For most of us, heaven is something that we have to inten-tionally set our minds on. It's worth it. The more we make heav-en our preoccupation, the more our lives become radically transformed. People, possessions, career, time, pain, and plea-sure all have meaning when viewed through the lens of heaven.

When our minds are set on heaven, a radical change occurs in our thoughts and attitudes. Hoping in heaven in the biblical sense is indeed transforming. As C. S. Lewis notes,

> Hope is one of the Theological virtues. This means that a contin-ual looking forward to the eternal world is not (as some modern people think) a form of escapism or wishful thinking, but one of the things a Christian is meant to do. It does not mean that we are to leave the present world as it is. If you read history you will find that the Christians who did most for the present world were just those who thought most of the next.[1]

The reality of eternity was the central motivation of the disci-ples during the early days of the church. The resurrection of Christ proved to them that heaven was real. Since there was life after death, nothing on this side could distract them. For them the other side was worth living for—and dying for if necessary. Nothing this passing world offered could deter them from living for eternity. Heaven was the primary reference point of their existence.

RIVETED TO HEAVEN

Making heaven our primary point of reference transforms us as well. What does it mean to make heaven our ultimate point of reference?

Points of reference rivet our attention and alter our behavior. When a college student prepares for a major grade-point-threatening test, he views all of life through the grid of that impending exam. If he neglects that point of reference—if he fails to prepare—he feels guilt and fear. If he gives proper attention to that point of reference, he will begin to do things he's never done before. He will say no to other less-important activities such as pick-up basketball and instead spend a long night at the library, sifting through his research notes and resources as though he were a scholar.

We all have points of reference. They dictate who we are, what we dream about, where we go, and what we do when we get there. Among these may be marriage, a vacation, a promotion, a baby soon to be born, a new home, a new car, retirement, a memory, an aged parent, ongoing sickness, or long-term sorrow.

Interestingly, life ultimately makes us somewhat cynical about our most anticipated points of reference since experiencing them is never quite as satisfying as we thought. Receiving an "A" on this exam soon becomes a distant memory with another exam to follow. We grow accustomed to a new house, and it's no longer new. A new car becomes used and out-of-date. Retirement becomes meaningless and depressing unless we discover new passions to spark our interest.

We experience a gnawing sense of incompleteness because we were built for something to look forward to, for something beyond ourselves, without which we are not whole. It is heaven for which we were built and redeemed. The disappointment we feel in earth-side experiences is an indication of heaven in our hearts.

Lewis again explains the issue well, writing:

> Most people, if they had really learned to look into their own hearts, would know that they do want, and want acutely, something that cannot be had in this world. There are all sorts of things in this world that offer to give it to you, but they never quite keep their promise.[2]

Heaven must become the target of our hearts. It's what we are meant to aim for.

An unalterable focus on heaven appears throughout Scripture. The first mention of heaven, though indirect, occurs in Genesis 3, when God promises Adam that one day his enemy would be defeated (verse 15. The first patriarch of Israel, Abraham, "was looking for the city which has foundations, whose architect and builder is God" (Heb. 11:10). Other references are more direct. David looked forward to seeing his dead son again (2 Sam. 12:23), and the psalmist could cope with the prosperity of the wicked because he knew his God would ultimately receive him into paradise (Psalm 73).

In the teachings of Christ our gaze is lifted toward heaven. In the writings of Paul, Peter, James, and John we read about a certain, future home. In Revelation, John rivets our attention as God judges Satan, sin, and sinners; destroys this present world and all that is defiled by sin; and in a glorious conclusion introduces the new heaven and the new earth and establishes the City of God as the centerpiece.

Once we are convinced of this glorious consummation of sin-defiled time, space, and history and are introduced to eternity and its heaven, we are never the same again. When seen in its all-encompassing reality, heaven quickly becomes our all-consuming point of reference. It looms above everything else, trivializing that which is earthbound and lesser.

RADICALLY ALTERED

When we make heaven our reference point, we will know it because everything on this side becomes radically rearranged. At least seven aspects of our lives become wonderfully changed as a result of setting "your mind on things above" (Col. 3:1–2).

Posture Toward God

First, *our posture toward God is radically changed.* We change from being temporalists—those consumed by the gain of the moment—to being eternalists—those consumed by the reality of God in eternity.

Remember the man who called to Christ from the crowd, "Tell my brother to divide the family inheritance with me" (Luke

12:13)? He had fixed his hope in life on the income from his inheritance, and his brother had not given him his share. Christ seized the moment and said, "Watch out! Be on your guard against all kinds of greed; a man's life does not consist in the abundance of his possessions" (verse 15).

Jesus then told the story of a man of great wealth (verses 16–21). To celebrate his success the man threw a party and invited all his friends to come. He commanded that they should eat, drink, and be merry. But, as Christ noted, a surprise guest came to the party: God. He said to the supposedly shrewd and successful man, "You fool!" He was a fool not because of all the stuff that he had in his barns, but because he was a *temporalist* rather than an *eternalist.* He had never thought of his life beyond this fleeting world. "This very night your life will be demanded from you. Then who will get what you have prepared for yourself?" (verse 20).

In this parable, Christ stretched this wealthy businessman's definition of life to include the reality of eternity, to the moment when he would present his soul to a holy God without the credentials of his earth-side success. That's a penetrating thought for all of us who have assumed that life derives value through an embossed title on a business card.

Millionaire Norman Miller, chairman of Interstate Batteries and a racing car enthusiast, has realized that, more than earthly success, he needs to be reconciled to the God of eternity through Christ. Having accepted Christ, he now runs his business with eternity's values in view. Norman sponsors a weekly Bible study held in the Dallas warehouse of Interstate Batteries, where drivers and salesmen also pray for a stronger commitment to Christ, their family, their country, and their job of selling automobile batteries.

Miller has made Interstate the leading replacement battery manufacturer in North America, with revenues of $350 million in 1994. And he is sold out to Christ. "I need to be faithful to Jesus 100 percent of the time," declares Miller. "And that includes my business."[3]

Perspective on Possessions

The second outcome of a life focused on heaven is *a proper attitude toward our possessions.* Christ indicates that fixing our hearts on heaven also will revise our perspective on our possessions.

The old bumper sticker is right: "You can't take it with you." It has been well said, "You won't find a funeral hearse pulling a U-Haul trailer." Heaven-convinced Christians regard everything they have on earth as an investment in heaven. Our possessions become not something to be stockpiled here, as symbols of our significance, but rather commodities to be used for eternal gain.

How do you view your time, talents, material goods, and finances? Are they commodities for your own consumption or capital that you can invest in eternal gain?

On October 27, 1993, a series of fires raged through parts of southern California, fanned by the notorious Santa Ana winds coming off the desert. One area hit especially hard was Laguna Hills, a beautiful upper-class community set inland from the Pacific Ocean. House after house was torched by the wind-swept blaze. Flames jumped from rooftop to rooftop, finding fuel in the cedar shake shingles.

After the fire swept through the neighborhood, only ash-covered foundations remained where scores of homes once stood. But there was one exception. The home of building contractor To Bui stood tall. The contractor wanted his home to last, so he had constructed the roof with concrete and tile. The fire tested the roof, found it inflammable, and skipped over it to others. In fact, newspapers across the country carried the dramatic photo of that one house standing amid acres of burned houses.

God's Word indicates that what we do here with all we possess will be evaluated at the bema seat of Christ. Like Bui, we want to be wise builders. We want to construct our lives out of materials that will stand the testing by the fires of judgment. When we enter His presence, the blaze of His glory will burn away everything that is not fit for eternity. Those activities and possessions won't necessarily be bad, just that which was merely earthbound in its nature. The only things of value, the only things that will remain, will be what we have done on this side that make a difference in the world to come.

Paul says our earth-side activities and resources that have been used for eternal gain will endure as though they were gold, silver, or precious stones. All other things will burn as if they were wood, hay, or straw (see 1 Cor. 3:11–14).

When we do not invest our possessions in eternal gain, we become what Francis Schaeffer called "ash-heap Christians." Such Christians don't necessarily live evil lives, but their stay on earth simply has no effect on eternity. Schaeffer noted that there will be many standing before Christ at the bema seat "knee deep in ashes with hands empty" of anything solid and worthwhile to bring to the Savior on that day.[4]

What earthly possessions do we have that can be used for gain in the world to come?

Let's begin with the people in our lives—our family and friends. Are we willing to give ourselves and those we love to honoring God *now* and telling others about the Redeemer *now*?

Edward, a student from the Ukraine, is studying at Moody Bible Institute so that he might go back and train other pastors and leaders in that needy land. As sometimes happens on college campuses, he has fallen hopelessly in love with a fellow student, Linda. She enrolled at Moody with a heart committed to serve God wherever He led her. She probably would have never dreamed that it would be in the Ukraine, especially given the tough living conditions there.

Edward and I chatted one day about his future, including his plans for getting married and then returning to serve Christ in his native land. "How is Linda feeling about it?" I asked.

With a glow on his face, Edward told me that she is happy and excited about the prospect. Her parents, however, are struggling with the idea of having their daughter go so far away. He added, though, that they had dedicated her to the Lord when she was a baby and were willing to release her to whatever God called her to do with her life.

Those parents have been liberated from the bondage of the earth-side pull of their most precious possession. They would love for their daughter to stay close to them and to see their future grandchildren grow up. But they recognize that those plans are less important than God's eternal cause. When they stand before Christ on that final day, the release and support of their daughter will turn into gold, jewels, and precious stones that are worthy of eternity. In fact, because they gave their daughter to an eternal cause, those jewels may very well be Ukrainian souls won for heaven.

Another possession we can invest in for eternal gain is our financial resources. Jesus commanded us, "Use worldly wealth to gain friends for yourselves, so that when it is gone, you will be welcomed into eternal dwellings" (Luke 16:9 NIV). The heaven-focused believer finds great pleasure in learning to use his funds to enhance and enrich eternity. I like to think of entering heaven's gates as people rush up to introduce themselves to me and tell how money I gave to God was used by Him to guarantee their eternity.

I believe that the life of our Messiah was spared in His infancy because three wise men during a brief visit gave their resources in worship to the King of kings. How else could Mary and Joseph, who were simple, common folk, be able to afford a long journey and residence in Egypt for two years to escape the wrath of a seething Herod who had decreed that all two-year-old boys throughout the land be killed?

Our possessions also include our homes. Russ and Beth Knight bought a small A-frame on the south side of Chicago as well as a piece of vacant land next door. They turned the land into a playground and their home into an after-school shelter for neighborhood kids. Today the playground is safe territory among the gang-ridden turf, and their home is a place where the love of Jesus Christ warmly welcomes city kids, whom they tutor after school. Their home and surrounding land demonstrate the eternal love of Christ to those who know little or nothing of true love, let alone the marvelous embrace of Jesus Christ. There is no doubt in my mind that Russ and Beth are using their home for eternal gain.

Time is an eternal resource. Teaching a Sunday school class can affect the life of a child who may positively affect the lives of others. We can devote our spare time to behind-the-scenes volunteer work, such as offering our skills in writing, nursing, or counseling to clinics in inner-city ministries, or simply stuffing envelopes or changing diapers in a church nursery. This kind of work may offer little recognition at present. But our efforts will surely initiate our heavenly focus and bring eternal gain.

Perception of People

The third result of keeping a heavenward focus is *a new perception of people.* Just before His ascension into heaven, Christ asked His followers to turn their hearts toward the people who did not know Him. He told them to await the Holy Spirit, and then to "be my witnesses in Jerusalem . . . and to the ends of the earth" (see Acts 1:3–8 NIV). Christ constantly elevated the value of people. And with good reason. People are the only things that will last for eternity.

Everything else stops at the border.

Our perception of people changes from their being commodities to being eternal creatures in need of the redemptive touch of God's grace when we view them through hearts hooked on eternity. We want them to join our pilgrimage and find their way to our eternal home.

If we believe that those around us are candidates for redemption and that we hold the key to their eternity in heaven, we will act and respond with unconditional compassion, generosity, and love. We will no longer see them as objects to be used, abused, manipulated, or consumed for our own pleasure.

A father who looks at his daughter with eternity in view would never abuse her with words that humiliate or anger her, or even consider abusing her physically or sexually, lest he build a wall between her heart and the redemptive work of Jesus Christ. With eternity in focus, business people would act ethically, both because it's right and because it allows them to open the heart-doors of people with whom they work—and even of those against whom they compete.

When our hearts are focused on heaven, crowds at major sporting events and in malls at holiday time become individual people —we begin to care about the eternal destiny of the guy cheering next to us or the rather weird-looking teenagers walking ahead of us. They become the focus of our prayer and compassion rather than a mass of irritating people who elbow their way in front of us.

Perspective on Pain

Fourth, fixing our minds on heaven *changes our perspective on pain.* Christ declared to John in Revelation, "Now the dwelling of God is with men, and he will live with them. They will be his people, and God himself will be with them and be their God. He will wipe every tear from their eyes. There will be no more death or mourning or crying or pain, for the old order of things has passed away. . . . I am making everything new" (Rev. 21:3–5 NIV).

When Joni Eareckson dove into a bay at seventeen and snapped her neck, her life changed drastically. This active teen who loved horseback riding suddenly became paralyzed from the neck down. In the midst of her despair and anger toward God, a friend named Steve Estes turned her heart toward heaven. Joni went through more pain during her rehabilitation, but with eternity waiting, she left the anger and depression and moved on. Today the promise of eternity is evident in her life. She is a blessing to believers and non-believers alike, to the disabled as well as the physically fit. Now married, Joni Eareckson Tada writes books and magazine columns and speaks before large crowds. Heaven often dominates the words she speaks and the pages of her books.

Ken Medema's gifted artistry as singer and songwriter belies the fact that he is blind. On one particular occasion he sat at the keyboard with Joni. "Joni, let me compose a song for us," he requested. As he sang to her of heaven, the notes included these words: "I can't wait to *see* you and have you *dance* in my arms."

African-American slaves were buoyed through the tragic and shameful pain of their plight by their belief in the reality of heaven. In fact, their labor was filled with hymns and spirituals reminding them that a better day was coming.

Whether our present pain is chronic or occasional, physical or emotional, one truth can help us endure: It's all temporary, soon to be replaced by a permanent, pain-free body. Placing our minds on heaven gives us the right perspective on pain.

As Martie and I often said during difficult days of parenting, "This too shall pass." If heaven is in focus, those words ring soothingly at the core of our being.

During his own difficult times, Paul wrote, "I consider that our present sufferings are not worth comparing with the glory that will be revealed in us" (Rom. 8:18 NIV). If we think that our

reward will be on this side of the grave, we will be easily discouraged and cease to persevere in doing what is right. But if
we know that what we do for Him here counts for eternity,
though the results may be unseen, we continue to steadfastly
carry on for Him regardless of our circumstances (see 1 Cor.
15:58). A clear view of the other side enables us to persevere on
this side.

My first visit to the former Soviet Union was just months after
the collapse of the Communist empire. I spoke at churches that
were filled with faithful saints. They had persevered through the
raging rule of Stalin when they had been relegated to peasant
status. Nearly all had been denied education and professional
advancement. Yet in spite of seventy years of oppression they
filled their churches and sang heartily of their love for God.

As they sang, the interpreter whispered the words to me. Like
the African-American slaves, many of their hymns were about
heaven. At the close of many services in Russia we stood together and the congregation sang a particular tune that was familiar to me. Though I didn't understand the Russian words, I
found myself singing along in English. As they sang, children
from the church came with flowers and presented them to us as
a farewell gift. During the last chorus my brothers and sisters in
that far land lifted their hands and waved farewell to us as they
sang:

> God be with you till we meet again;
>   till we meet,
>   till we meet at Jesus' feet;
> God be with you till we meet again.

In the midst of their suffering, heaven had become clear and
compelling. The song was a sign of heaven in their hearts.

One of the last regimes to fall in Eastern Europe was the government in Romania led by the ruthless dictator Nicolae
Ceausescu. The flashpoint of his overthrow occurred when a
pastor, Laslo Tökes, refused to obey politically motivated orders
to leave his church and take an assignment elsewhere. He
stayed inside the church building, and his congregation surrounded the building with their own bodies, creating a human

shield against the security forces who sought to take the pastor prisoner.

Most of these Christians did not fear death, even when the soldiers threatened brute force. They were, after all, bound for heaven. What did the temporary loss of life matter? Their courage and faith were too much. The soldiers could not—they would not—challenge these people and their pastor.

This event was the flashpoint that finally led to the toppling of Ceausescu and his regime. Interestingly, the song of the revolution that filled the streets was a hymn of the Romanian church. Its words proclaimed the victory of the second coming of Jesus Christ. It had been their hallmark in dark and terrible days when they were called on to suffer much; and now it would be their victory song as the hope of their freedom dawned.

Throughout the history of the persevering church, courage in times of pain has been grounded in the reality of heaven. When threatened, heaven-focused Christians knew that dying was gain; when their treasures were taken they were not shaken because true treasures are in heaven; when threatened with torture they bore up under it, knowing that the sufferings of this present time are not worthy to be compared with the glory that shall be revealed on the other side.

German theologian Dietrich Bonhoeffer, when he was led to be hung for his commitment to righteousness in the face of Nazi atrocities, confidently spoke these last words: "Oh, God, this is the end; but for me it is just the beginning."

Pleasures on Earth

The fifth outcome of a heavenward focus is *enhanced pleasures on earth.*

When we experience the pleasures that this world offers, they are soon mere memories. Yet, for us who are mindful of heaven, they remind us that the brief pleasures we experience here only foreshadow the fuller, more exhilarating eternal pleasures that await us.

Our earth-side pleasures may include a good meal, a great party, an evening with friends, a good book by the fire, a walk through the country with spring in the air and flowers along the path, or a faithful dog. Clearly, the depth of these pleasures cannot compare to the ongoing pleasure that we will have from His right hand forever. We enjoy pleasures now as merely a foretaste of what is to come.

Our most anticipated pleasures here are often tainted with less-than-expected results.

When Disneyland first opened on July 17, 1955, everyone was excited and wanted to get in. Walt Disney and his staff had sent out invitations to 20,000 special guests—politicians, celebrities, the press, and Disney studio employees. Somehow more than 10,000 uninvited guests were also able to get in with counterfeit passes. By mid-morning, Mickey, Donald, and Goofy were mingling with more than 35,000 children and adults.

Walt called his place the Magic Kingdom, but that first day was anything but magical. When the park opened, cars stretched bumper to bumper for seven miles along the Santa Ana Freeway southeast of Los Angeles. Refreshment stands quickly ran out of supplies. Long lines of cranky visitors formed outside the few operating rest rooms. The Mark Twain steamboat nearly capsized on its maiden voyage. Walt Disney later called the day "Black Sunday."

Now, forty years later, Disneyland has spawned its bigger cousins, Disney World (Orlando), Euro Disney (Paris), and a Tokyo version as well. It has revolutionized amusement parks. And of course, the opening day mistakes were temporary. Disneyland today is a model of order, cleanliness, and fun. It's become almost everything a child could imagine such a place would be.

But at the end of the day, kids and parents go home exhausted, having spent themselves in long lines and crowded rides. The pleasure, as wonderful as it was, is but a memory.

In heaven we will experience "pleasures forever," untainted, unspoiled, and far beyond our expectations.

Purity

The sixth outcome of a mind set on heaven is *a life committed to purity here.* As John notes, "Everyone who has this hope fixed on Him purifies himself, just as He is pure" (1 John 3:3). Recognizing that our souls are eternal, we realize that on earth we are grooming our real selves for heaven. With a mind focused on that eternal union—a final reunion with a God who is absolutely holy and a Savior who is wholly pure and could return at any moment—we feel an urgency to be ready with purity in our hearts.

Every bride wants to be ready for her wedding day. She knows that the best gift she will give the groom is herself—her body, her mind, and her heart—and she wants to be pure and beautiful for him. She spends months preparing for that moment when the organ calls her down the aisle to her husband. She searches for just the right dress and spends hours on her hair and cosmetics. To these add the radiance of her joy, and she appears in unparalleled beauty.

In Jesus' day, the Jewish marriage custom required that the groom go to the bride's father and establish the price for gaining his bride. The father and the future husband sealed the covenant with a cup shared between them. The groom would then leave for a lengthy period, returning to his father's home where he prepared an apartment that would become their home.

Then, without announcement, when everything was finally ready and the wedding feast prepared, he would leave his father's home and walk through the streets of the town to receive his bride and take her home. As he walked, his wedding entourage would shout in the streets, "The bridegroom cometh!" People drawn from their homes would gather in a swelling crowd, shouting the good news. The bride, hearing the shouts from the streets, would meet him at her home and go with him to the feast and to their new home.

Needless to say, there was no time to prepare herself for that great celebration if she waited to hear the shouts in the streets. Given that her hope was fixed on that day, she had already prepared herself in anticipation of his coming for her.

So it is with us whose hearts are fixed on that day, when the trumpet will sound and our bridegroom, the Lord Jesus, will finally come to take us home. Those who live in the context of the reality of that hope live here preparing themselves for there.

When we remember that we will be asked to give an account there for all that we have done here, heaven motivates us to purity.

Sense of Identity

The final outcome of a mind focused on heaven is a transformed sense of identity. Scripture has two identifications for home-bound believers: (1) we are *citizens* of that other land who demonstrate the distinctives of the world to come; and (2) we are *aliens* and *strangers* in this world.

Paul describes us as citizens of heaven in Phil. 1:27–28 and 3:17–21. He tells us as citizens of the celestial city to "conduct yourselves in a manner worthy of the gospel of Christ" (1:27).

Citizens bear the telltale marks of the culture to which they belong. As Christians, we are to bear the identity of the culture of His kingdom which is to come. The kingdom virtues mark us as belonging to heaven just as clearly as my friends from Memphis are marked by their thick southern drawl.

The second proper perception of ourselves is that we don't belong here. We are *aliens* and *strangers* on earth. We may find fulfillment and pleasure along the way, but we're just passing through. Let's say your destination for a summer vacation is the Grand Canyon. You may be able to enjoy the trip, with a smooth ride and new sights along the way, but your focus is on that final destination. All you do and the decisions you make along the way are determined by that destination. That, after all, is where you belong at a certain time. Everything else is interesting but secondary to arriving at the rim of the canyon, looking across the chasm and down on the Colorado River and exclaiming, "I'm finally here! What a view! It was worth the trip."

Scripture deals with this issue of belonging through several word pictures. No longer strangers and aliens toward God, we are now strangers, aliens, and exiles of this earth.[5] These are pilgrim words that indicate, as one scholar put it, "someone who lives for a short while in a foreign place."[6] *Strangers* have no long-term ties; they are in transit. Their lives stand out by the distinct differences of the culture to which they belong.

Aliens have a unique perspective of possessions. Although they may own things along the way, all these things become dispensable in light of their destination. They recognize that ownership is temporary, so they hold things loosely and share them with those in need (1 Tim. 6:18). Their possessions become instruments of fairness and righteousness (Lev. 25:23). King David, a man of great wealth, reflected on his pilgrimage in a prayer of thanksgiving before God, noting,

> Wealth and honor come from you; you are the ruler of all things. In your hands are strength and power to exalt and give strength to all. Now, our God, we give you thanks, and praise your glorious name. But who am I, and who are my people, that we should be able to give as generously as this? Everything comes from you, and we have given you only what comes from your hand. We are aliens and strangers in your sight, as were all our forefathers. Our days on earth are like a shadow, without hope. O Lord our God, as for all this abundance that we have provided for building you a temple for your Holy Name, it comes from your hand, and all of it belongs to you. (1 Chron. 29:12–16 NIV)

The pilgrim mind-set, best exemplified by Abraham (see Heb. 11:8–10), recognizes that as aliens we don't belong here and that we live seeking the country to which we do belong.[7]

To claim a pilgrim's identity means that we always know we're not home yet. For us the best is yet to come. Therefore, everything is expendable here, free to be used for the glory and gain of the King.

Living in the reality of heaven has tremendous relevance. When we envision heaven as our home, everything in life is radically rearranged. It affects our posture toward God, our possessions, people, pain, and pleasure. And heaven in our hearts purifies us and alters our sense of identity.

If we say we believe in heaven, then let's show our redemptive passport. Let's look at the ledger of our checkbooks and the pages of our Day-Timers.® Do we see heaven in how we view and treat people? Is there peace in the midst of pain? Do earthly pleasures stimulate our hearts toward a thirst for pleasures forevermore? Let's check the purity of our souls and our identity as pilgrims rather than permanent residents.

When heaven is the habit of our hearts we love more freely, worship more deeply, share more gladly, and suffer and sacrifice more readily. When the other side is real, everything on this side is radically, wonderfully rearranged.

What then does it take to make heaven a habit of our hearts?

CHAPTER NINE

THE HABIT OF OUR HEARTS

PUTTING HEAVEN IN ITS PLACE

A s our children were growing up, periodically in moments of weakness I would say to them, "Marry for money; you can learn to love." Needless to say, I wasn't serious. In fact, we tried to keep the emphasis in our home on issues of faith in Christ and character in life. Nevertheless, there is a principle hidden in that rather pagan perspective: Some of the most important traits in life can be learned and cultivated through a focused effort.

For centuries in most cultures, marriages were not the result of a spontaneous, youthful attraction, but rather they were pre-arranged by parents long before the children were of marrying age. Many of those marriages were highly successful because, in the course of living together, the couple committed themselves to learn to love each other and to build positive and constructive responses to each other—at first intentional and then, over time, natural and spontaneous.

MIND TRAINING

In a very real sense, lives that are transformed by making heaven the primary point of reference are lives that have been *trained* to occupy themselves with the world to come. A life fixed on heaven is not instinctive. After all, we were born blind to heaven and dead in our hearts toward God. Many of us have long years of blindness to overcome. Through all the early formative years and then the critical choice-making years, neither heaven nor God ever played a part in our thoughts, choices, or affections.

Even those of us who grew up in Christian homes and heard Jesus' name and periodically heard of heaven have not trained our hearts to be preoccupied with paradise. As C. S. Lewis noted, "We have not been trained: our whole education tends to fix our minds on this world."[1]

Complicating our quest is the fact that this present world is so tangible. It is so touchable, seeable, and enjoyable that even with the Spirit stirring in our hearts, we may very well be distracted by it. We must consciously choose to listen to and obey the Spirit's prompting. And we must train our hearts to see beyond this world into the next.

The missing emphasis on heaven and eternity in our churches does not help. So much of our focus remains on meeting people's earth-side needs, finding the right programs. No wonder many think that heaven is a P.S. on the Christian experience rather than the heart of it.

And, while biblical therapies and earth-side strategies are important, we desperately miss the perspective that heaven brings. Heaven is the only place of full and final healing and fulfillment. A heaven-oriented point of view also realizes that at times God permits us to be less than fully healed here. He often desires through our sorrows to accomplish things that could in no other way be accomplished for His glory.

If heaven is not at the core of our ministries, then not only do we have a limited view of the fullness of life and our redemptive experience, but we are unable to help those who are in need. Often the eclipse of heaven in our hearts merely reflects how our good intentions have become swallowed in a tidal wave of pressures. Though we know that heaven is important, and we want it at the center of our existence, we find that the gravity of this world pulls us back.

HEAVEN ON OUR HEARTS

Making heaven the habit of our hearts is not just something that would be nice—it is necessary. Without heaven in our hearts, we jeopardize our relationships, our careers, and our consciences. A heaven dimly lit results in a life poorly lived.

What would it take then to learn to fix our hearts on heaven? To long for the other side so that it becomes the overwhelming point of attraction and attention; that it becomes the transforming power of our lives?

John Goddard has allowed one final destination to affect his life here. His destination is what he calls "My Life List." The list contains 127 goals. At age fifteen, Goddard sat down at a kitchen table in Los Angeles and began writing goals on a yellow pad of paper; he labeled the page "My Life List." Since then he has completed 108 of the goals.

The goals aren't simple or easy. They include climbing the world's major mountains, exploring vast waterways (such as the Nile, Amazon, and Congo rivers), running a mile in five minutes, reading the complete works of Shakespeare, and reading the entire *Encyclopaedia Britannica.*[2]

How did Goddard accomplish so many of these amazing goals? By fixing his attention on the final destination of completing his list.

The fiery eighteenth-century preacher Jonathan Edwards is probably most remembered for his frequent emphasis on hell and in particular his sermon "Sinners in the Hands of an Angry God." But he would be remembered by his parishioners in the North Hampton, Massachusetts, church by his references to the hope of a heavenly destination. He often told them, "This life ought so to be spent by us as to be only a journey towards heaven."[3] In a message preached from Matt. 6:21, he emphasized, "'Tis a thing of great consequence to men that their hearts should be in heaven."

What would it take then to make heaven a habit of our hearts?

Heaven as a habit of our hearts first requires a mental shift. As Paul commanded, we are to "set [our] mind on the things above, not on the things that are on earth" (Col. 3:2). The transforming power of this shift is evident in the proverb "As he thinks in his heart, so is he" (Prov. 23:7 NKJV). Thoughts set on heaven will lead to choices that reflect heaven, choices that "seek first His kingdom" (Matt. 6:33). Heaven prompts choices that reflect a readiness for His return. Christ Himself instructed the disciples to set their minds on heaven (see Luke 12:31–40). He urged them in the light of eternity to "be dressed ready for service and keep your lamps burning, like men waiting for their master to return from a wedding banquet, so that when he comes and knocks, they can immediately open the door for him. It will be good for those servants whose master shall find them ready." Heaven on our minds will trigger choices in our lives for which we will be glad to give an account, for which we will be rewarded.

PROGRAMMED BY PARADISE

When Paul challenged the church at Colosse to "set your mind on the things above, not on the things that are on earth," he was not asking them to maneuver through life in an ethereal daze with eyes glazed over, meditating only on what it would be like when they finally got home. He was calling them to think from heaven's point of view.

The word that Paul used for *mind* in verse 2 was used in the language of his day to describe the actual content of one's thoughts, not the thinking process. When it comes to computers, I'm relatively illiterate, but I know the difference between how a computer processes by means of chips, floppy disks, hard drives, megabytes, etc., and the programs you insert into the computer. The entire output of the computer is dictated by the software programs. Using a computer program for word processing won't do you any good if you want to do your budgeting on that computer. For that you'll need a program called a spreadsheet. You must change to accommodate the desired outcome. That's exactly the concept that Paul is speaking of here, that we program our minds toward things above so that all of the output of our lives reflects heaven.

That requires us to stretch beyond the immediate mental limitations of earthbound perspectives, to a broader mental context—one in which the realities of heaven and eternity frame our thoughts and conclusions.

OUT OF BODY REALITIES

The first programming change is to realize that while I am physically earth-side, spiritually I am already with Christ in heaven (Eph. 2:6; Col. 3:3). As such I have full access to the throne of God and communion with Him and His Son Jesus Christ through the Holy Spirit. That means heaven and eternity function right now as present realities.

We typically think of heaven as what comes next. While that is true for us in terms of where we dwell, it is not true that heaven is a future reality in terms of our present existence. Heaven is now. It is a real place now where God the Father and His Son Jesus Christ and the numerous angelic hosts reside. Compared with eternity, life on this planet is merely a blip on the screen. In the never-ending span of eternity, heaven is an ever-present reality.

As a present reality and the location of the Almighty God who created this planet, heaven has values we are to embrace. When we set our minds on God, we set our minds on His values. We focus on His character as well as His vision for our future. This heaven-oriented programming of our minds brings out thoughts consistently in line with His thoughts, and we will love what He loves and hate what He hates.

PERKS OF PARADISE

A heaven-oriented mind-set such as this offers three important benefits to our lives.

Security

The first comes from the understanding that we are hidden with God in Christ until the day of our full redemption and entrance into heaven. The truth is, we are fully secure in this life. You or I could lose everything in this world, and yet be fully certain about the world to come. Such certainty shelters us from consuming despair. As Paul writes triumphantly: "For I am convinced that neither death, nor life, nor angels, nor principalities, nor things present, nor things to come, nor powers, nor height, nor depth, nor any other created thing, shall be able to separate us from the love of God, which is in Christ Jesus our Lord" (Rom. 8:38–39).

Stability and Supply

Second, realizing that heaven is a present reality where I am "hid with Christ" assures me that I have an intercessor, Someone who is ready and able to meet my spiritual needs. As our intercessor, Christ is like the high priest of Old Testament times. In fact, Jesus is actually called our high priest (Heb. 4:14–16). In the Old Testament era, the priests were the mediators between God and man. They represented the Jewish people to the God of Israel. They approached Him much as an attorney approaches a judge today in representation of his client; they represented the Israelites' needs to God. By having a high priest as a spiritual intercessor, the Jews could hope for cleansing and forgiveness, as well as for the grace of God on their lives in the time of their need.

Unfortunately, by the time Christ came, the offices of high priest were bought and sold in the political arenas of Rome, and these wealthy priests had little contact with and virtually nothing in common with the average Jewish worshiper. They created a phenomenal distance between themselves and the people. When the priest exercised his priestly functions, the Jews of Christ's day felt that, though there was liturgical representation, the priest had little personal understanding of their needs before God.

However, we have a High Priest in heaven who is far different. He was tempted in all points like we are, yet was without sin (Heb. 4:15). He can intercede for us as a high priest because of His own righteousness before God. Having fulfilled the sacrificial requirements to make us acceptable to God the Father, He presently represents us in heaven on an ongoing basis, securing our acceptability before the Father through His death on the cross. Christ is our compassionate Mediator. As Hebrews says, we can come boldly to the throne and find mercy and grace to help us in our time of need through Christ who functions right now as our priest in heaven. When our minds are set on this reality of heaven, we maintain stability in our souls regardless of what is happening around us. When we feel lonely, rejected, misunderstood, taken advantage of, we know that He has felt it all before and that He understands and readily supplies grace and mercy. When pain is our portion—when weariness, thirst, and hunger are our companions—we know that He has been there before and that He cares like no one else can care.

As a small boy growing up in Hackensack, New Jersey, not many miles from New York City, I remember sliding my pillow over to the side of the bed late on some nights and turning on my little radio. After my dad prayed with me, turned out the lights, and shut the door, I'd listen to "Big Joe's Happiness Exchange." The program beamed from the heart of the city. I realize now that the show must have encouraged many lonely, hurting individuals. As a boy, it brought great comfort to me at night.

The program always began with a deep but mellow and tender voice saying, "Have no fear, Big Joe is here." He then sang this song:

> Somebody cares about you and worries
>   till the sun comes shining through;
> Somebody cares if you sleep well at night,
> If your days go all wrong or your days go all right.
> Please believe me, it's so, but in case you didn't know it,
> Somebody cares.

Big Joe then began to field telephone calls from people in the city who were hurting. With an understanding and quieting spirit he would talk to them and help them. If they had material needs, other people would call in to offer help. When a mother couldn't afford to have her refrigerator fixed, for instance, a caller would offer an appropriate replacement. That radio program in effect was a citywide expression of grace and mercy in a time of need.

As uplifting and refreshing as "Big Joe's Happiness Exchange" was, we have an intercessor who does far more as our High Priest. He is just as caring as Big Joe, but much more powerful and knowing, and He is glad, willing, and able to be personally involved in our present spiritual needs.

Advocacy

The third privilege of setting our mind with Christ in heaven is that we become assured that He is presently defending us against the accusations and attacks of the adversary. In 1 John 2:1 we are assured that presently in heaven "we have one who speaks to the Father in our defense" (NIV), someone who is "an Advocate with the Father" (NASB). This advocate is "Jesus Christ, the Righteous One."

In Rev. 12:10, Satan is seen as the accuser of the brethren. As Satan challenges us before the throne of God, Christ actively defends us because He has covered us in His righteousness and our sins have been forgiven by the atoning work of the Cross.

When the throne room echoes with charges against me, Christ rises to attest to the Father that His shed blood has covered all my sins.

In a court of law, having an advocate is essential. In fact, it's a right to which even the poorest of defendants are entitled. Most public defenders embrace their roles. Several years ago a Cincinnati attorney, appointed to defend a man accused of burglary, surprised the judge by asking to withdraw from the case. But the attorney had a good reason. His own office had recently been broken into, and the person he was named to defend had been indicted for that crime. The judge agreed that as a potential victim of the defendant, that attorney could not fairly defend a suspect accused of forceful entry and burglary.

Surely Jesus has been sinned against by each of us, yet He gladly has agreed to be our advocate. Furthermore, most attorneys lose cases at times. Innocent men are convicted because of tired or poorly prepared advocates. Unlike such advocates, Jesus is a strong, wise, and caring advocate who brings our requests to the Father. He never loses a case.

In addition, right now in heaven Christ is restricting the work of Satan against us. As is clear from Job 1, He stands as the sovereign sentinel at the gate of our lives permitting only those things that He can turn to His gain or glory. His present work in heaven guarantees that in every trial of life He will make a way of escape that we will be able to bear it (1 Cor. 10:13).

For all of us who think that God hasn't done much for us lately, we might remember each night when we put our heads on our pillows to thank God for what He did for us that we knew nothing about; for the defense that Christ gave to us in the courts of heaven when we were accused and assaulted. When the adversary seeks to destroy me, heaven is busy with the edict of the Father who guarantees the outcome. When He allows me to walk through the valley, heaven sends a flurry of angels who bring me His grace as an act of His mercy. They camp around my life to protect me from ultimate destruction. As the psalmist says, "The angel of the Lord encamps around those who fear Him, and rescues them" (Ps. 34:7).

Those of us who set our minds on things that are above live with a sense of undaunted security and confidence, knowing that we are right now hidden in heaven in Christ. We recognize that we have a High Priest who understands our weaknesses and happily sends us grace as an act of His mercy in the time of our need. Finally, we feel security and safety from knowing that right now an advocate and defender is acting on our behalf.

The authentic, effective believer is one who lives with his head in the clouds.

THE CHARACTER OF PARADISE

Col. 1:2–3 calls us to not only set our minds on things above but to seek that which is above as well. What is above? What should we seek? Heaven is a place where righteousness, justice, compassion, and forgiveness prevail. In heaven love, purity, patience, and wisdom are at work. In heaven God's sovereignty, power, and all-consuming love prevail.

Think of how different our lives would be if our minds were programmed with this kind of data from above. How quickly and spontaneously we would delight to worship Him. We would obey and follow Him regardless of the possible consequences. We would love instinctively, as He loves. Justice would characterize our lives, and we would display His righteousness in acts of mercy and grace. If the things of heaven make up our mind, then our lives will both know it and show it.

ETERNITY

THE ALTERNATIVE

If we do not set our minds on Christ and all that is in His heaven, we are left to focus on earth. There is no middle ground. When we understand the characteristics of an earth-side mind-set, however, we know how risky it is to let our minds stay earthbound. Paul, in describing typical secularists and counterfeit religionists, describes them as being "enemies of the cross of Christ, whose end is destruction . . . whose glory is in their shame" (Phil. 3:18–19).

Look at where earth-side thinking has taken our society. In the final decades of the twentieth century, America is more desperate and frustrated than ever before. The weight of unsolvable societal problems is crushing our national spirit. We find ourselves asking, *How did we get here from there?* We can trace the decline to our university campuses where academic leaders began to propagate the theories of rationalism and relativism, which in essence say that there is nothing supernatural and nothing that is absolute—nothing is always wrong, nothing is always right. Rationalism and relativism leave no room for a righteous God and the reality of heaven. We were left to ourselves without God and an eternal home. Like children left at home alone, the results have been devastating.

Earth-side philosophies soon gave rise to what we call pluralism —the idea that everyone is entitled to believe whatever he or she wants to believe. Men and women are entitled to claim their own view of truth about themselves and life in general.

As a result of such "modern" thinking, tolerance has now become the highest value in our culture. Since nothing is right or wrong and in essence all are entitled to define what is right and wrong for themselves, we must be willing to believe that what everyone believes is equally valid. And as long as it does not hurt or violate someone else, we must tolerate whatever someone chooses to do. And so each year about 1.5 million unborn children die by abortion. Variant sexual choices are offered to our children via the blackboards and video screens of their health and sex education classes in public schools. In the name of tolerance prayer has been taken out of our schools and condoms have been put into the schools.

Many secularists celebrate this as a season of enlightenment in America; they call it progress and say, "Our minds have finally been liberated from the shackles of the old Victorian, Judeo-Christian mind-set. Now we are free to think and do as we see best." But the devastating outcome of a world with no God and heaven to hold us accountable is measured in an increase in crime, disease, substance abuse, and overall instability. Without God there is no solution, only increasing despair.

Unlike those who make choices based on this world's value system, authentic Christians fix their hearts and minds on eternity and make choices based on heaven's value system.

HAVING A HEART FOR HEAVEN

But it's not just where we park our minds and hearts. It's where we place our affections as well. We are naturally drawn to those things we feel affectionate toward. And it is these bonds of affection that preoccupy our hearts.

I met Martie in the fall of our freshman year at college, and it didn't take long for me to know that my heart had become hopelessly lost to her. We dated throughout the remainder of that year. When summer came she went home to Cleveland and I went on the road for two and a half months with a team of musicians representing Cedarville College. I traveled with four other students, playing in a trombone trio and doing some preaching. All of us had become friends during the year as we prepared for the summer and ministered in churches on weekends. We had a great summer, with lots of exciting experiences, interesting places to travel, and chances to meet all kinds of people in many different churches. But no matter how new and exciting the trip was, no matter how satisfying the ministry seemed, my mind kept returning to Martie. I would hope there would be a letter from her at the next church we visited. I hoped she would be home when I called. I wondered where she was, what she was doing, and what we'd be doing together if she were with me. And needless to say, I was looking forward to the day that our itinerary would bring us back together again.

It's like that for those of us who are developing an ever-deepening relationship with Jesus Christ. We increasingly love to read His mail to us—the Word of God. In Scripture we hear from Him, find out more about Him, and sense comfort and direction in His words to us. And we increasingly enjoy our times of prayer, when we can speak with the Father directly and sense God's communion with us.

There are many reasons our hearts are drawn to our eternal home. Perhaps in heaven we will reunite with a spouse, a child, a parent, or a dear friend. In heaven we will also leave behind the troubles and heartaches of life. Indeed, the more troublesome our environment and the more complex our crises become, the more we long for home.

But the compelling attachment of my affections for heaven is the presence of Christ and the promise of an eventual reunion with Him, the lover of my soul.

DIRTY WINDOWS

My friend Bud Wood is the founder and developer of what has become one of the finest homes in America for mentally challenged children and adults. Shepherds Home, located in Union Grove, Wisconsin, ministers to many who are afflicted with Down's Syndrome. The staff at Shepherds makes a concentrated effort to present the gospel to these children. As a result many have understood and come to believe in Christ as Savior and in a heaven that will be their home.

Bud once told me that one of the major maintenance problems they have at Shepherds is dirty windows.

"What? How could that be a problem?" I asked.

"You can walk through our corridors any time of the day," Bud explained, "and you will see some of these precious children standing with their hands, noses, and faces pressed to the windows, looking up to see if Christ might not be coming back right then to take them home and make them whole."

Their simple minds and hearts have much to teach us. We should be asking ourselves, *When was the last time we glanced toward the sky to see if this might not be that long-awaited moment when we finally see Him face-to-face?*

When Paul said being in heaven was "better by far," he said it in the context that heaven meant being with Christ (Phil. 1:23). Remember, from God's creation of man and woman, God has made us to have fellowship with Him and His Son. The joy of

Eden and that initial paradise on earth was focused on the relationship that Adam and Eve had with the God of the universe. That relationship brought them a fullness of satisfaction and unlimited pleasure in God.

God longs for us to be restored to Him and His fellowship. He finds pleasure in us. Only men and women were made in His image. He put a piece of Himself within us. He has made heaven for us so that we can finally, forever dwell with Him.

Isn't it true that relationships are our most treasured possession? Massive doses of material goods, thrill-a-minute entertainment, education, and professional advancement mean little. And in fact, without positive relationships, they can bring additional pain.

When we cross the border and enter His presence, all the darkness of this world will be left behind. He will fill us like we've never been filled with an unhindered relationship with Him. Imagine the unparalleled moment when we experience the brilliance of His welcoming presence and the sight of His Son, the crowned King of kings.

A GOOD HABIT

Making heaven the habit of our hearts involves training our thoughts and affections to mimic the ambience of heaven—its persons and practices. When God's Word talks about the heart, it refers to who we are when all the veils are stripped away, layer by layer. It is the authentic me. Scholars note that the term "heart" means "the place in us where we dream, deliberate, decide, and desire."

Thus, the heart is the arena where all of life is determined. When we give our hearts, the authentic us, to heaven, our lives will reflect the reality of that choice.

Making heaven the habit of our hearts is without a doubt the most important habit we will ever cultivate. And when heaven becomes our habit, we will no longer be carried through life by the past or even the present, but by the blazing lights of Edenland that dawn on the horizon.

My grandfather served as a pastor in Jackson, Michigan, for more than thirty years. He went home to be with the Lord just after his ninety-fourth birthday. I remember a few years earlier sitting with him in church one evening before the service began. He told me that he didn't sleep much anymore and often woke up in the morning around 4:00. I asked him what he did in those early hours.

"Usually I just lie there and think."

"Think about what?" I asked.

"I find myself thinking about how wonderful it is going to be to go home and be with the Christ I have served and grown to love. I've lived a long and good life, but the best is yet to come."

He knew heaven was real, that Christ was there, and that with absolute certainty based on Christ's finished work on the cross and the empty grave, there was one final stop for him: the other side. He would soon be home, and for him that was certain and sure. It consumed his mind and captured his affections.

His love for heaven stamped a legacy on my heart. I find myself praying that I will never be so distracted that heaven becomes dimmed or eclipsed by the lesser things in this present world.

When heaven is in our hearts we will look forward with hope to the day when we will emerge on the other side.

PART THREE
THE ETERNAL WORLD WITHIN

It is not enough to think of the world to come in future terms. Eternity has been born within our hearts. The reality that it has come to us making us representatives of the kingdom of eternity is a transforming truth.

For the redeemed, the world within is no longer managed and manipulated by the forces of this present world but by Christ, the conquering King of the world to come. As Scripture affirms, "He delivered us from the domain of darkness, and transferred us to the kingdom of His beloved Son" (Col. 1:13).

CHAPTER TEN

THY KINGDOM COME

CHANGING PLACES

W hen the Willises called a press conference two days after their devastating minivan fire on that Milwaukee bypass, they epitomized the very essence of believers who biblically embrace a three-world view. In that news conference, they made a conscious choice to reenter the arena of the fallen world that had victimized the most sacred treasures of their lives.

Simply fading into the background and waiting for heaven to be home was not an option for them. Sinking into the despair of this world was inconceivable to them. Instead, they built a platform in the midst of this fallen world from which they could express the empowering reality of the kingdom of Christ. The essence of the kingdom of Christ is *righteousness* and *conquest*. They righteously proclaimed the truth that their God was still a good and loving God, and they waved the flag of conquest in the face of the adversary who sought by this tragedy to embitter them and embarrass the name of Christ.

When crisis is our lot, one of the most common flaws among those of us who claim His name is our tendency to shrink into the background, bemoan the awfulness of the world, and either find our spirit embittered or enraptured with dreams of the world to come. God never intended for us to be sidelined by tragedy in this present world. Our redemption has placed us into the kingdom of Christ. That kingdom was intended to be a righteous force in this world as a symbol that this world's system will someday be conquered by our King.

Nobody proved that point better than the Willises.

We are, above and beyond everything else, citizens of the kingdom of Christ—the kingdom within our hearts. And as such, it is our responsibility to manage His kingdom within in ways that are consistent with the righteous victory of His kingdom.

ETERNITY IN OUR HEARTS

Although the redemptive world within is distinct, it is not divorced from the world to come. In fact, there is an inseparable link between them. The link is Christ, the eternal King who reigns in our hearts now and who will reign throughout eternity. In a very real sense, heaven—in terms of its unique culture, principles, protocol, and practices—is being born within us. It is our privilege to express its future glory through our lives here and now.

His kingdom within us should make everything different. How we think, live, act, and respond should be shaped by the birth of the eternal kingdom within. This new world within is managed and directed by Jesus Christ. My life is the *realm* over which He *reigns*. Like distinct colonies in a foreign land, our lives are expressions of His kingdom here and now. Those of us who are driven by the identity of the kingdom within live by a different and unique authority. We yield our lives gladly and unquestionably to the authority of Christ the King. As such, all that we are is radically altered and our lives offer a compelling glimpse of heaven on earth.

Living in a democracy places us at a disadvantage. We elect our leaders. They serve at our pleasure. If we don't like them, we wait for the next election. But we can't transpose the democratic mind-set to the kingdom of heaven. You and I did not elect Christ to rule as King. Nor does He rule to please us. Nor will we wait four years from now to elect somebody else to be king. He is King. As such He ultimately rules over all the affairs of mankind. And in particular He reigns over those who are members of His kingdom.

The clearest statement of our kingdom relationship to Christ is framed in Col. 1:13 where we read that God has "delivered us from the domain of darkness, and transferred us to the kingdom of His beloved Son."

THE ATTITUDE OF GRATITUDE

There are several strategic elements for us to note in regard to our kingdom status. Kingdom people live with an unconquerable sense of *gratitude*. Paul states that in light of our deliverance, we are to give thanks to the Father who made our citizenship in the eternal kingdom possible (Col. 1:12).

Given the alternative, you can see why. Our existence is rooted either in the "domain of darkness" or the "kingdom of His dear Son." The domain of darkness is a phrase that describes the destructive grip that Satan has on all who are not redeemed. The word "domain" refers to the realm over which He reigns. His realm is characterized by darkness, which is a reference to the forces and realities of evil that are void of the light of God's truth and power. It is also significant to note that the word "transferred" literally means "to be rescued, released from bondage." In a redemptive mission of deliverance, Christ has released us from Satan's grip and granted us protection under His reign.

When the text states that God "delivered us out of the domain of darkness," it uses a word that most often refers to someone who delivers a person out of a situation over which he is unable to deliver himself. In fact, in classical Greek, this word *deliver* refers to the pagan Greek gods who were the only ones able to deliver the imprisoned from their plight. We are thankful recipients of God's rescuing grace. If it weren't for His initiative and sacrifice, we would remain in the fatal grip of the evil one.

Born into the domain of Satan, we were hopelessly trapped. The only light at the end of the tunnel was the judgment of God heading straight for us. There was nothing we could do. An understanding of our bondage to the domain of darkness is noted in Ephesians 2 where we are called *dead* in sin. Death separates us fully, and we are unable to prevent its damage.

But I fear that we take our privileged place in the kingdom too easily for granted. We assume that one day we realized our bondage to sin and sought a Savior, as though we had done the good deed. We enjoy the privileges of the kingdom with little sense of gratitude and no thought of our indebtedness to Him.

Paul Harvey tells a great story about the Italian sailing team racing in the America's Cup. The race this particular year was held in Australia. On one of their days off, the Italian team decided to rent a Jeep and go into the outback to enjoy the scenery and see if they could get a glimpse of a kangaroo or two. The team had been completely outfitted by the Italian designer Gucci. They wore Gucci jackets, carried Gucci bags, and wore Gucci watches.

As they were driving through the outback, a kangaroo hopped in front of them. Unable to stop the Jeep in time, they hit the kangaroo and it fell on the road in front of them—apparently dead. The team members all jumped out to take a look. Someone suggested, "Let's at least take a picture!" The driver suggested, "Before we take the picture, I'll put my jacket on it so it looks like even kangaroos wear Gucci clothes!"

They put the jacket on the limp animal, and as they stepped back to take the picture the kangaroo suddenly revived and hopped into the brush—wearing the jacket! Unfortunately the driver's keys and wallet with his American Express card were in the jacket! I can just hear the other kangaroos: "Hey, where'd you get the Gucci jacket? Keys to a Land Rover! An American Express card?!"

All that to say that even those of us who have a measure of theological sophistication might assume that at one point we came to our senses about God, were spiritually revived, and hopped back to live in this present world with all the privileges of heaven and the potential of Christ in our possession.

It didn't happen that way! We were dead—hopelessly, helplessly lost! Condemned! In bondage to the darkness of this domain. Ultimate despair and death were all we could look forward to in the future. Then God the Father called us, and by His marvelous grace He touched us. By His sovereign power He made us alive in Jesus Christ, rescued us from enslavement to the adversary of our souls, and placed us in the kingdom of His dear Son. When we are tempted to become nonchalant about our kingdom world within, we must *stop* and think of the significance of being fully delivered from the domain of darkness.

I love Paul's statement to Timothy. Paul instructs Timothy to gently correct those who oppose the gospel so that "if perhaps God may grant them repentance leading to the knowledge of the truth, they may come to their senses and escape from the snare of the devil, having been held captive by him to do his will" (2 Tim. 2:25–26). Note that it is God who gives a spirit of repentance, raising our awareness of sin, that starts the process of release. Without this gift of grace all of us remain in Satan's snare.

CHANGING PLACES

Not only is gratitude the compelling theme of kingdom hearts, but a kingdom person has a clear sense of his or her *place* in this world.

We have not only been gratefully delivered from Satan's realm, but the text indicates that we've been transferred to Christ's realm. The word *transferred,* in Col. 1:13, refers to the completeness of the rescue in terms of a secure place in Christ's kingdom.

One of the great tragedies after the Emancipation Proclamation was that so many of the freed slaves had nowhere to go. In fact, many of them opted for continued slavery rather than deliverance to nowhere in particular. Our Deliverer gives us a place to belong. We have been transferred to the best place possible: the kingdom of "His dear Son."

In earlier days, when a conquering king took an empire, he would create colonies in the new territories. The people in these colonies were granted citizenship in the new ruler's empire with all its privileges and responsibilities. God has colonized us into His kingdom and delivered us to live as unique communities of belief representing the King of the world to come in the midst of this pagan world.

Some of us carry passports that identify us as citizens of the nation to which we belong. The symbol and name of one's nation is proudly displayed on the cover of that passport. As kingdom people you and I live on this planet, but we claim citizenship in another land.

KINGDOM LIVING HERE AND NOW

As believers, we have no more important identity than kingdom citizens.

Yet many of us struggle with this identity. As we have noted, most of us do not live in "kingdoms." We live in democracies and are taught the importance of personal independence and self-determination. Living for ourselves is preeminent. Living under the authority of another is an alien thought—a thought that causes some tension. It is critical then that we transition our thinking to effectively understand and express the reality of our kingdom identity.

Obviously, this kingdom has a King. The King is Christ who has an undisputed right to rule and reign. And it's a kingdom with subjects—real subjects, you and me.

Our experience as subjects of this kingdom will be realized in three distinct phases. The final phase is the eternal world that is yet to come, heaven. We will revel in the eternal kingdom of God, unthreatened by Satan and the forces of this present world. But before that kingdom is inaugurated, Scripture indicates that there will be a literal kingdom of Christ on this planet, when He will reign in person for one thousand years. At that time Christ will fulfill His promises to Israel, and we who are redeemed will reign with Him in our resurrected bodies free of sin and self, gladly doing the will of our King and reflecting the character of His kingdom (see Revelation 20).

But before these eternal and millennial phases of this kingdom, there is a *present* sense of the kingdom. I like what John Eadie says in his Greek Text Commentaries concerning Col. 1:13:

> The "kingdom of His Son" is plainly that kingdom which has Christ for its head and founder which is partially developed on earth and shall be finally perfected in heaven. . . . It belongs, of right, to His Son. Christ founded it, organized it, rules over it, prescribes its laws, regulates its usages, protects its subjects, and crowns them with blessings. It is therefore a kingdom of

light whose prismatic rays are truth, purity, and happiness. . . . This kingdom is one which the Colossians belonged to at the period of Paul's writings. It is a present state, but one which is intimately connected with futurity.

In this present world, you and I are not only people of the world to come, but of a kingdom that exists within us at this moment. This kingdom within affects the farthest reaches of our life: our behavior, attitudes, actions, and responses. We are citizens of this kingdom, and it is our primary identity on earth.

THE KINGDOM PAST, PRESENT, AND FUTURE

To enhance our capacity to embrace the kingdom as an active force in our lives, let's trace its fascinating development from the beginning of time all the way into eternity. In the beginning God created an environment where He reigned in unquestioned authority. His kingdom provided complete satisfaction, fulfillment, and fellowship for Adam and Eve. The realm was beautiful beyond description. Their worth and dignity were undiminished. They found satisfaction in their relationship with the Almighty God of the universe and pleasure in their responsibility to care for their environment on His behalf. God found pleasure in them and their obedience. Adam and Eve were built for this marvelous relationship and found significance in the experience.

Then Satan came and lured them with promises of more than he could offer. Satan knew that if he could capture the appointed governors of this planet he could make it his domain and use it as a platform to deface God's glory and defame the Creator's name. All of creation was a visible manifestation of God's magnificent glory, and having been created in His image, man was the pinnacle of it. If Satan could capture them he could place disorder in the place of order, pain in the place of joy, ugliness in the place of beauty, death instead of life; and by doing so discredit God. If he could infiltrate the planet with greed, self-glory, manipulation, and treachery, then God's name would be in jeopardy. If life could be driven by pride, focused on self with passions consumed with selfishness, then all of hell could rejoice in the demise of God's glorious landscape.

Like a jealous child who steals and destroys a friend's new toy, Satan sought to steal and destroy all that God had created. He succeeded, the domain of darkness captured Adam and Eve, and the stage was set for Satan's brutalizing work.

At this point God could have annihilated all of creation and moved on to another project. Instead, God chose to rescue what was lost. And over the stretch of millenniums He has patiently moved toward total victory over Satan, one redeemed person at a time. Toward the creation of a new heaven and a new earth where, like Eden, fulfillment and satisfaction will be complete in Him. But unlike Eden it will be a place where there will be no possibility of failure or loss. It will be a perfect place ruled by a perfect God populated with redeemed people who experience unhindered joy and satisfaction in His presence. It will be a place eternally free from sabotage since the enemy of our souls and his ghoulish hosts will be eternally bound in hell. In this place the ravages of our enemy—death, sorrow, crying, and pain—will be unknown (Revelation 19–21).

How will all of this come about? In order to assure a safe eternity, Christ has been appointed to finally defeat Satan and to deliver to God the completed work of victory over our adversary. This conquering, completing work of Christ is *the* agenda of His kingdom.

The first reference to an eternal kingdom where Christ rules is given in a promise to King David: "Your kingdom shall endure before Me forever; your throne shall be established forever" (2 Sam. 7:16). It becomes increasingly clear as the Old Testament unfolds that God would send His Son as the Messiah to be conqueror and eternal King.

Before the assignment of Christ to be King, however, there were earlier references to God's full and final victory over Satan. In Gen. 3:15 God promised that the seed of woman would bear a child who would inflict a fatal wound to Satan's head, though Satan would inflict a nonfatal wound to the child of the woman.

Then God promised Abraham that in him all of the families of the earth would be blessed (Gen. 12:3). His child Isaac gave birth to Israel, who was the progenitor of twelve sons who would form the nation that bore his name—the nation through which the Conqueror would come. The conquering work of the

Messiah as King is heralded in passages such as Psalm 2 where God's begotten Son is granted final power over the rebellious nations of the earth.

Through Christ's extensive and authoritative teachings, the New Testament underscores the centrality of the kingdom. The kingdom's importance is reflected as well in the disciples' expectation that Christ would overthrow the oppressive rule of Rome, establish Himself as King, and plant His eternal kingdom on earth. Their limited perspective hindered them from seeing beyond their temporal needs to a better kingdom when Christ would return and reign on this planet for a thousand years as a prelude to the eternal reign of God after Satan's final judgment and doom in the lake of fire. Throughout Acts the central theme of the preaching of the early church was the proclamation of the kingdom. (See Acts 8:12; 19:8; 20:25; 28:31.)

KINGDOM CONQUEST

It is important to keep in mind that the immediate purpose of Christ's kingdom is conquest. Paul writes in 1 Corinthians 15:20–26:

> But now Christ has been raised from the dead, the first fruits of those who are asleep. For since by a man came death, by a man also came the resurrection of the dead. For as in Adam all die, so also in Christ all shall be made alive. But each in his own order: Christ the first fruits, after that those who are Christ's at His coming, then comes the end, when He delivers up the kingdom to the God and Father, when He has abolished all rule and all authority and power. For He must reign until He has put all His enemies under His feet. The last enemy that will be abolished is death.

According to this text, when Satan is finally defeated, Christ will transfer His kingdom to God who will reign eternally with Him in a better place called heaven. We who are now part of Christ's kingdom will at that point be finally and securely transferred to God for His eternal glory and our eternal joy. Until then we remain subjects in the kingdom of His dear Son and as such a part of Christ's conquest. We serve the purpose of the King and the kingdom every time we say no to temptation; lead someone to Christ; give Him full control over everything in my realm to be used for His glory and gain. There is no greater privilege than to participate with Christ in His work of conquest. It is the most important cause in history.

Conquest over sin and Satan is living proof that we have changed places, from the domain of darkness to the kingdom of His dear Son.

Not only have we changed places. We have changed identities as well.

CHAPTER ELEVEN

KINGDOM TRANSFORMATION

CHANGING IDENTITIES

reat ideas, major corporations, and well-funded endeavors all depend on capable management. Only strong management can help a company reach its maximum potential. Lee Iacocca demonstrated this when he took the floundering Chrysler Corporation and through visionary management transformed it into a viable force in the automotive industry.

Given the importance of Christ's kingdom in biblical history and its central task of conquest, how do we manage this kingdom world within, maximizing its full potential? What does it take to reflect the reality of this world within to a watching, wondering world?

As we have noted, all we are and all we have comprise the realm of His reign. The New Testament calls us His *body*, His *church*. Both images reflect His rightful authority and our glad submission to being used by Him to accomplish His ultimate purpose. Managing this process is our privilege.

There are two vitally important aspects of the kingdom that we must embrace if we are to manage our lives as effective subjects of the eternal world within. In fact, we will not be able to express the reality of the kingdom until we have understood and implemented both of these realities.

First, we must ignite the transforming power of perceiving our *primary identity* in terms of our place in the kingdom. Second, we must live within the boundaries of the *responsibilities* of the kingdom community as well as to value and enjoy its *privileges*.

KINGDOM IDENTITY

Our government spends millions of dollars each year in its witness protection program to change the identities of those whose lives are endangered. They are relocated, given a new name and identity. Having been relocated into the kingdom we too have been given a new identity—and, I might add, at a great price. Embracing this new identity is the first step in managing our place in the kingdom. Understanding who we really are transforms all that we do.

In *The Crimson Tapestry,* a novel by Michael Joens, Worm is a beggar who cares little for himself and even less for others. He is intelligent but uses his brain to plot schemes to deceive the townspeople to gain food and goods for his survival. As an orphan, he never knew his real name and was told that his stubborn warrior father caused the Saxon tyranny in southern England. The villagers told him as a small child, "Let the memory of [your father's] name be cursed forever, and you with him. Go away, child of the street . . . you are no longer welcome here. . . . Your inheritance is shame, you vile and despicable worm."

Thus driven from his homeland, Worm becomes a beggar in order to survive. As a teenager he uses his cunning for his own gain. One day, though, Allyndaar, a friend of his father, delivers Worm from the streets, and Worm discovers his true identity. He is the son of Caelryck, a noble warrior. Caelryck had learned to forge steel into strong swords, shown strength and bravery in war, and died nobly in battle.

"Your father was a great man," the friend tells him. "Britain lost her most valued son when he died." As Allyndaar tells Worm about his father, Worm begins to change. He learns his real name is Aeryck, son of Caelryck. His father is a hero to all who truly oppose Saxon oppression in England. Allyndaar and his family ask Worm to live with them and join the fight to maintain the Britons' freedom. And Worm, the beggar boy, accepts the offer. In a moving ceremony he receives his dead father's sword and eventually becomes a mighty warrior in the kingdom.

What brought about this radical change for Worm? His new identity came from learning that he was part of a noble kingdom and the son of a noble warrior. As the son of Caelryck, Worm became Aeryck, changing his identity and dramatically altering his life. As Christians who are heirs to the kingdom of Christ, we too are children of the conquering King. We bear his name and our new identity radically changes our lives.

THE DEFINING DIFFERENCE

The enemies of Christ use the hypocrisy they see in so many Christians to discount the claims of Christ. This is often a smoke screen to excuse their rejection of Christ. Do they really expect perfection from God's people? Even the secularists periodically contradict their own philosophy of life. Yet the stinging charges, more often than not, are well-founded. We possess an uncanny ability to reflect inconsistently the uniqueness of Christ's kingdom. Uncanny because the uniqueness of Christ's kingdom defines the difference between those who are heaven-bound travelers and those who are not.

Too often we have defined the difference between "us and them" in shallow, inconsistent codes of behavior. For instance, in days gone by, the distinctions of a Christian often focused on a list of those things to avoid: Don't drink, dance, smoke, chew, or go with those who do. The model of what it meant to be a Christian looked something like this: Be faithful to church, tithe, avoid doubtful work on Sunday. As important as they may have been, these lists often distracted us from the authentic distinctions of our identity in Christ, giving us a false sense of spiritual accomplishment. Satisfied that we had conformed to the list of dos and don'ts, it became easy to ignore the more genuine marks of eternity—the habits of heaven that make us truly unique.

Today in our more *liberated* Christian environment where many have discarded codes of behavior that smack of *legalism*, we continue to miss the genuine marks of eternity. Values such as generosity over greed, servanthood over self-centeredness, people over things, the eternal over the temporal, and pleasing God over self-satisfaction still elude us. We are short on kingdom traits such as compassion, truth, and the importance of a consistent and compelling testimony. All of these are unique characteristics of a life ruled by Christ, not driven by a sense of responsibility but rather by a glad preoccupation with our eternal identity.

Let me explain.

THE POWER OF SELF-PERCEPTION

As the story of the unfortunate boy called Worm affirms, our identity is a driving force in the formation of the kind of people we ultimately become. Many factors influence how we will perceive our identity: our gender; our professions, whether doctor, lawyer, butcher, baker, candlestick maker; our titles as mother, father, teacher; and our social status—rich, poor, blue collar, white collar. All these factors determine what we wear, where we live, how we speak, and the political and social perspectives we embrace. In addition, our ethnic identities define us with distinctives in dress, music, and culinary preferences.

The writer of Proverbs wrote, "As [a man] thinketh in his heart, so is he" (Prov. 23:7 KJV). While we often relate that proverb to good and bad thoughts, it is also true that the way we think about ourselves will ultimately define how we live. If this is true, then the way we think about ourselves can motivate us to live in ways that consistently reflect the kingdom of eternity in our hearts. Rarely do Christians perceive themselves in terms of a kingdom identity; hence, we are rarely known for distinctly kingdom behavior.

If you and I met and I asked you, "Who are you?" you would likely describe yourself in terms of your earth-side identities. You will rarely if ever hear anyone respond, "I'm a citizen of heaven, thanks for asking" or "I thought you'd never ask . . . I'm a subject of Christ's kingdom." Needless to say, it may be too pretentious to blurt out something like that, but the problem is not that we don't say it . . . we never think it.

If our kingdom identity doesn't preoccupy our minds, it will never define our lives. And if it doesn't define our lives, then we are vulnerable to the shifting influences of lesser identities that can lead to hypocritical behavior and an embarrassing contradiction of the kingdom within.

For instance, if you are a doctor and that identity defines your awareness, you may focus on living up to the image of a doctor. Social prestige may make you vulnerable to pride. And while these things are not in themselves wrong, professional expectations for expensive houses, cars, country clubs, and private schools could be the controlling force in the dispersal of your resources. A doctor whose identity is earthbound may find it difficult to give up a thriving practice to serve the poor in an impoverished neighborhood. Yet a kingdom identity would at least permit that to be an option.

In the tough Lawndale neighborhood of Chicago, Wayne Gordon, a white, and Carey Casey, a black, lead a ministry that is effectively demonstrating the love and transforming power of Christ. There are several doctors who have left their practices and their comfortable neighborhoods to move into Lawndale to operate a medical clinic alongside Wayne and Carey. It is clear that these doctors are driven by a sense of kingdom identity, which releases them to serve the less fortunate with the long stretch of eternity and the sake of their King in view.

Dr. Viggo Olsen was an agnostic at the pinnacle of his medical career when redemption revolutionized his life. His soul was not only rescued from hell, but his focus shifted to the values of eternity. He headed for Bangladesh and in the heart of the strongholds of Hinduism and Islam founded the Christian Memorial Hospital. He wrote a best-selling book some years later called *Daktar*. Many professionals in the medical field have accepted Christ as a result of the book. And it has prompted hundreds of others to commit their lives to serve Christ in foreign lands. Dr. Olsen's life is truly driven and defined by his kingdom identity in Christ.

TRANSFORMATION

Embracing our true identity in Christ revolutionizes our perspective on everything. Parenting becomes a platform from which to serve eternal realities. Children, in a kingdom perspective, are not extensions of our dreams or enhancements of our image. Rather, they are individuals reared to make valuable contributions to eternity. This means that as parents we seek to instill in them the virtues and practices that are consistent with kingdom behavior. If they live out these righteous qualities in their lives, they will be ready to make a contribution to glorify the King we serve. Thinking of children in terms of their contributions to eternity means that we will help them see that the choices they make for their lives are not merely opportunities to make money or even to make us proud parents, but rather platforms to advance the kingdom of their Father in heaven.

Parents who have a kingdom identity will be pleased with their children when they live godly lives and use their calling in life to please the King.

Students who have embraced a kingdom identity see their studies in light of the eternal truths of their eternal God. They see His fingerprints in the study of creation, biology, anatomy, geography, and astronomy. History becomes the story of the sovereign direction of the King. Mathematics, physics, and geometry reflect to them the fact that the world is governed by the laws that were instituted by the King. Arts and literature reflect the creativity God has placed within us, as we are made in His image. Philosophy, political science, and behavioral studies are evaluated in terms of the principles and perspectives of the kingdom. A student with a kingdom identity sees education from the King's perspective and is committed to developing his or her mind for maximum use toward the eternal goals of the kingdom. A future career is a launching pad for kingdom gain.

A kingdom perspective never lets us see our career as a means to self-gratification and personal advancement, but rather as a platform from which Christ is consistently seen and from which His work is advanced. We choose not to compromise the kingdom value of integrity for a raise or promotion, displaying to all that the kingdom is not about wealth and power but about righteousness and peace.

Retirees who live in their kingdom identity will not envision their remaining years reclining on a chaise lounge but rather investing their wisdom, accumulated goods, and skills to advance the cause of Christ. They will live with an awareness of their privileged place in His kingdom and volunteer their time and talents to Christian organizations or in their local church. Short-term missionary stints are an exciting and enticing kingdom option for retirees.

Grandparents who have found their identity in eternity are committed to spending time with their grandchildren, to help support their children in rearing a new and godly generation.

Racial tensions are defused in a mutual acceptance of identity in Christ. While politically correct agendas encourage us to reclaim our ethnic identities and find expression in our ethnicity, Christ's redemptive identity takes us beyond that to the overriding identity of our relationship to the King of eternity. Our identity in Him moves us across racial lines, where all of God's people share identity in the kingdom of Christ. We are not red and yellow, black and white. We are brothers and sisters in the kingdom. As Tony Evans says, "We may have all come over on different boats but we're all in the same boat now." I have often felt that those who are unwilling to accept those who "are not our kind" will have a lot of trouble in heaven, since some from every tribe and nation will be there (see Rev. 5:9–10).

Being preoccupied with our eternal identity not only levels the ground across ethnic lines but across socioeconomic lines as well. This present world has established a status for certain cultural distinctives such as race, physical appearance, career, power, and position. If in a social setting someone says "I'm a pipe fitter" and another says "I'm an attorney," the attention usually focuses on the more *prestigious* profession. But a relationship with Christ as King puts all of us on equal footing. We are all glad subjects in the kingdom, serving His glory and the advance of His cause, whether pipe fitting or litigating legal issues. How we function on this planet is seen in the light of who we *really are,* not on what we *do.* In a world that celebrates power, riches, health, comfort, and tolerance, Christ's sense of kingdom identity forced Him to conclude in the Sermon on the Mount that the poor in spirit, the grieving, the disempowered, and the righteous were truly blessed. This is why Paul reminded us that in Christ, "there is neither Jew nor Greek, there is neither slave nor free man, there is neither male nor female; for you are all one in Christ Jesus" (Gal. 3:28). In light of the fact that our lives have been changed by our identity in Christ, Scripture claims that we have been "crucified with Christ; and it is no longer I who live, but Christ lives in me; and the life which I now live in the flesh I live by faith in the Son of God, who loved me" (Gal. 2:20).

When I accepted the invitation to serve Christ at the Moody Bible Institute, a friend said to me, "You really took a step up!" He obviously had not yet been gripped with a sense of kingdom identity. There are no "steps up" in the kingdom. There are only servants who are sovereignly assigned to strategic places in the vineyard. This sense of identity unifies us as one in Him.

When we commit ourselves to our eternal identity in Christ, our lives begin to be transformed to consistently reflect the kingdom. Who are you? If you answer instinctively in terms of your place in His kingdom, if you think of His right to reign over your life, then you will display for all to see the reality of eternity. Our kingdom identity is a transforming reality.

But a clear sense of identity is not the only key to the effective management of the kingdom within. An appreciation of our privileges and a conscious embrace of our responsibilities is critical to the process as well.

CHAPTER TWELVE

KINGDOM PRIVILEGE

THE PERKS AND WORKS OF THE KINGDOM

W e all desire to be included in significant groups. I'll never forget the family trauma that preceded my daughter Libby's tryout for cheerleading. When she made the cut we all breathed a collective sigh of relief, and we basked in the privilege as well. I heard myself on several occasions say, "We have a daughter who's a cheerleader. . . ." But for Libby the privilege also brought responsibilities. She was expected to be faithful to practice, loyal to the other cheerleaders and the sponsor, and a good representative of the squad.

Every privilege in life brings its rewards and its responsibilities. Unfortunately, we are too often prone to consume the privileges and ignore the responsibilities. A kingdom citizen doesn't have that luxury. The King is worthy, and the cause is too important.

Our honored place in the kingdom bestows three special privileges and calls us to fulfill three specific responsibilities.

THE PRIVILEGE OF SIGNIFICANCE

I don't know of a more powerful urge in the human experience than the desire to count for something; to be affirmed; to sense with assurance that we have observable worth and dignity. Adam and Eve were built for significance. Their significance, however, was not in what they did. It was in the fact that they were created by God in His image and enjoyed an intimate, highly valued *relationship* with the great God of the Universe. In fact, He had trusted them with the *privilege* of managing and overseeing all that He had created. There is no higher sense of significance than to be accepted and affirmed as an intimate friend of God and to be trusted by Him to care for all that He has created.

Why do we delight in dropping names of important people we know and are associated with? Because our identity with them—their friendship, acceptance, and approval—gives us a sense of significance. Why do we strive for highly respected positions in our careers? Because we think that significance is related to what we are entrusted to do. The source of significance for Adam and Eve was their *relationship* with God and their *position* over creation. It is our privilege to have been restored to such a significance through the redemptive work of our King.

Our problems start, however, when we seek to satisfy this created impulse for significance apart from God and the responsibilities He has given us. This unfortunately leaves us vulnerable to a host of failures that instead of bringing enhanced significance bring hollowness, shame, and regret. Why do we boast? Slander? Gossip? Lie? Cheat? Violate our integrity in the marketplace? Spend too much time at the office? Overspend on houses, cars, and clothes? Secretly indulge in affairs that violate faithfulness to our spouses and our God? We are vulnerable to all of this because we assumed that we could find significance in ourselves and our pursuits apart from God. And, just as Adam and Eve, we ultimately feel shame and regret in the pursuit since there is no significance apart from a relationship to the only significant entity of the universe and a responsible stewardship of what He has given us.

Upon our transfer into the kingdom of His dear Son, we are fully restored to a *relationship* with the Creator of the universe and trusted by Him to carry out the *responsibilities* of the kingdom. This is a restoration to a secured sense of significance. For kingdom persons, significance is not a search. It is fully secured. It is a kingdom privilege. Since our significance is complete in Him, we no longer need to search for it in destructive activities. No amount of personally gained significance in terms of the passing wealth, fame, power, and position in this world can compare to being a child of the eternal King and belonging to the unconquerable kingdom of the Christ before whom all the significant powers of this world will ultimately bow their knees (Phil. 2:9–11). Even those who are thought of as significant from the world's point of view find significance only in Him, and those of us who feel less-than-significant in this passing world are fully significant in Him. We are all the same. We are all satisfied in Him and because of Him.

My dad was the most important thing in my world as a boy. He was the pastor of a large, successful church, a good preacher, a kind and gentle leader. His gifts were recognized by several boards upon which he served. He was a household name in our denomination. Wheaton College recognized his stellar service to Christ with an honorary doctorate when he was in his early forties. People would often say to me, "Oh, you're Joe Stowell's son" or introduce me as "the son of Dr. Stowell." I was proud of my dad and so honored to be his son that to be known as his child was a sufficient source of significance. I was happy and satisfied to find my significance in him.

That is but a glimpse of what it means to be satisfied with the significance that comes with being a child of the King. There is no greater honor, affirmation of worth and value, or earthbound significance that can compare. When we understand and claim this kingdom reality for ourselves, we are released from the competitiveness of trying to establish our worth and place in the heap of humanity, and we are wonderfully released to carry out the responsibilities He has given us to glorify Him and serve the gain of His kingdom. I am obviously not free to do that if my need for significance is driving me to glorify myself and live for the gain of my own kingdom.

THE PRIVILEGE OF SECURITY

Second, being preoccupied with our kingdom identity grants the privilege of an unflinching *security* at the very core of our being. Most of us struggle with a variety of insecurities. Insecurity haunts us when we are all alone, in social settings where others intimidate us, and in environments where more is expected from us than we can deliver. In professional environments we are compared to more effective, efficient people.

When a horrific explosion rocked the Murrah Federal Building in Oklahoma City in April 1995, people realized that their safety is not guaranteed by living in the heartland of America. More than 160 died and 400 were injured when a bomb hidden in a rented truck sheared the front of the building. Among the dead were more than one dozen children, found in a day-care center on the second floor.

"We really thought we were twenty years behind the big cities in crimes and mayhem and hatred," said Oklahoma City attorney Jon Casey, himself injured in the blast. "But now we know we're really in the same country as New York, Chicago, and Los Angeles." A sociology professor at the University of Washington added, "We are now finding out that no one is safe anymore, and they are astoundingly frightened."[1]

The bomb, believed to be set by domestic militants, shook buildings up to forty miles away. Newspaper analysts argued that the blast also shook the innate confidence of parents that their children were safe in public buildings or even private day-care centers. Across the nation, parents of preschoolers felt insecure. Brenda Lopez of Chicago, with her two children ages four and five at her side, expressed parents' fears when she told a reporter, "You [now] think, 'It could happen any day. Anywhere.'"[2]

This world is an insecure place. We cannot depend on social or financial success—or even location in the heartland of America —for security from life's setbacks. But we can feel safe from lasting insecurity as we realize that we have been eternally placed in the kingdom of Christ. The kingdom provides a secure environment that assures us of security during life's fleeting traumas. We can feel secure in the face of comparison and intimidation when we happily accept our identity as the King's children and find pleasure in serving the King as we are, where we are, knowing that He is pleased when we are faithful, loyal subjects of His.

Our sense of security is bolstered by the fact that the kingdom is a safe place to dwell, and all who are transferred into the kingdom find ultimate safety in the King. We are securely, eternally members of His kingdom. Christ spoke of this safety in John 10:27–30 when He promised, "My sheep hear My voice, and I know them, and they follow Me; and I give eternal life to them, and they shall never perish; and no one shall snatch them out of My hand. My Father, who has given them to Me, is greater than all; and no one is able to snatch them out of the Father's hand. I and the Father are one." Paul reiterates the theme in Rom. 8:35–39:

> Who shall separate us from the love of Christ? Shall tribulation, or distress, or persecution, or famine, or nakedness, or peril, or sword? Just as it is written, "For Thy sake we are being put to death all day long; we were considered as sheep to be slaughtered." But in all these things we overwhelmingly conquer through Him who loved us. For I am convinced that neither death, nor life, nor angels, nor principalities, nor things present, nor things to come, nor powers, nor height, nor depth, nor any other created thing, shall be able to separate us from the love of God, which is in Christ Jesus our Lord.

There is no more powerful King than Christ, and He keeps His citizens safe to Himself and for Himself.

Our place in His kingdom is also secure. As strong as Satan is, he has no capacity to take us back to the eternally damned domain of darkness. In fact, the Spirit of God has been assigned to guarantee our safety. Paul notes in Eph. 4:30 that He has sealed us unto the day of redemption. The word "seal" was a word familiar to Paul's readers. It meant the imprint of the king's ring on an edict from the king. The seal guaranteed its completion. This sense of ultimate security enabled Paul to say, in the face of the pressures from this fallen world that would destabilize anyone's sense of security, "We are afflicted in every way, but not crushed; perplexed, but not despairing; persecuted, but not forsaken; struck down, but not destroyed" (2 Cor. 4:8–9).

Even death cannot shake us of this security, for it only means a fuller realization of the privileges of the kingdom. For kingdom people "dying is gain."

We are secure from Satan's sniper fire. He cannot deliver a fatal shot. While we will experience the ambush of the adversary, the King always stands as the sovereign sentinel at the gate of our lives letting in only that which can be turned ultimately to His glory. Even in Satan's ravaging attack on Job, the King of glory stayed Satan's hand to guarantee the accomplishment of His divine purposes. We have a King who works *all things* together for good (Rom. 8:28)—a King whose safe protection guarantees that "no temptation has overtaken you but such as is common to man; and God is faithful, who will not allow you to be tempted beyond what you are able, but with the temptation will provide the way of escape also, that you may be able to endure it" (1 Cor. 10:13).

A PRIVILEGED FREEDOM FROM DESPAIR

Third, a firm embrace of the reality of our identity with and our place in the kingdom assures freedom from a prevailing sense of despair. I don't know that there has ever been another generation that has grown up with a greater sense of despair. When you listen to the music and read the writings in our pop culture today, it's evident that this generation feels phenomenal measures of meaninglessness. Is it any wonder? This generation will reap the epidemic of AIDS. They've seen the potential of nuclear holocaust. We've told them about holes in the ozone layer and global warming. Even in the body of Christ there is despair—despair over what has happened to our country. "Everything is sliding away . . . we've left the Judeo-Christian base . . . what will we do?"

In Scripture the reality is that since Christ is King and since He rules and reigns, there is no need for us to despair. Ultimately and finally God will bring resolution to all that is on this earth. In Psalm 11 the psalmist asks, "If the foundations are destroyed, what can the righteous do?" (verse 3). The psalmist states that we should not "flee as a bird to the mountain"! Don't retreat! Don't be in despair! But rather we should be confident that the eyes of God are upon the wicked and that He notices and rewards the acts of the righteous.

Christ is seated on His throne as King. His kingdom will mature into the kingdom of eternity, where despair will be finally and forever defeated. By redemption you and I have been transitioned from the hopeless despair of the domain of Satan. Even death, the ultimate stroke of despair, holds no sway over us. Scripture tells us in 1 Cor. 15:20 that death is the ultimate stroke of Satan. It is fascinating that the despair of our culture is so deep that we now celebrate death as a valid solution. Our pop and rock music emphasize this concept. Suicide is promoted as a valid life option. Abortion is demanded as a societal right. Euthanasia advocates like Dr. Kevorkian market death as a legitimate resolution of our despair.

Every difficulty, every pain, and every agony we experience are just the initial blows of the ensuing reality of death against us. It is Satan's ultimate stroke against God's created, material order. There is no victory against despair in ourselves alone. Not one of us can stay its agony unless we are part of the kingdom of Christ who will reign and rule as King until He has put away the final enemy, death, and then present the kingdom to God, the Father of eternal life. The King cancels the power of despair! No wonder Scripture says, "O, death, where is thy sting? O grave, where is thy victory? . . . Thanks be to God, which giveth us the victory through our Lord Jesus Christ" (1 Cor. 15:55 KJV).

But it is not just these privileges that are ours as kingdom persons. Our responsibilities are equally important.

WE PLEDGE ALLEGIANCE

Living out our kingdom identity demands that we accept our responsibility to grant the King our non-negotiated *allegiance.* The very fact that He is the eternal King (1 Tim. 1:17) gives Him the right to supreme authority over all that we are and all that we have. It is supreme arrogance to think that Christ—who created the entire universe through His spoken word, who conquered the forces of hell through the Cross and Resurrection, who has been granted by the Father the divine right to rule the kingdom of which I have been graciously included—has no right to total control in my life. It would be especially strange to deny Christ complete allegiance when we read Paul's effusive list of the credentials that establish our King's supremacy:

> for He delivered us from the domain of darkness, and transferred us to the kingdom of His beloved Son, in whom we have redemption, the forgiveness of sins. And He is the image of the invisible God, the first-born of all creation. For by Him all things were created, both in the heavens and on earth, visible and invisible, whether thrones or dominions or rulers or authorities— all things have been created by Him and for Him. And He is before all things, and in Him all things hold together. He is also head of the body, the church; and He is the beginning, the first-born from the dead; *so that He Himself might come to have first place in everything*" (Col. 1:13–18; italics added).

While the whole fallen world vests authority in the individual by encouraging us to "do our own thing" or to claim with Frank Sinatra "I did it my way," the believer who has come to grips with his or her identity in the eternal kingdom knows the privilege of saying yes to the King. Gladly. Unquestionably. Consistently. Regardless.

RESPONSIBLE CONQUEST

And, living as loyal subjects to our King, the second responsibility of the kingdom traveler is to contribute to the goal of the kingdom: *conquest.* This issue is at the heart of the kingdom itself. As we have noted, the purpose of Christ's kingdom is the final, ultimate and unchallenged defeat of Satan. Christ's purpose is to remove any threat of invasion or sabotage by the adversary for eternity. Until that final moment when our King has "put all enemies under His feet," Satan continues to create skirmishes on the borders of our lives. I'm convinced that he seeks to use our lives as platforms where he can demonstrate his power and bring shame and discredit to the name of the King. But the heart of the kingdom is the defeat of Satan. We reflect the glory of the King's power and the central work of the kingdom when we marshal the forces of our hearts, minds, and strength to demonstrate the conquering power of Christ the King.

We do this by submitting to the authority of the King. Every time I say yes to the King, Satan is defeated again. Temptations of greed, gain, sensual satisfaction, pride, and the illegitimate use of power create arenas for us to demonstrate our allegiance to the King. To say to the adversary in the face of attack "I would rather serve the King than reach for what you offer" leads us to conquest in even the strongest attacks. Though it is always a struggle, it is just as simple as that.

It is a privilege as a kingdom person to carry the flag of conquest as an early warning to the enemy that his doom is sure. As Martin Luther said, "One little word shall fell him." For kingdom persons that word is "yes" to the authority of the King.

KINGDOM CONFORMITY

The third kingdom responsibility is *conformity* to the culture of the kingdom. There is a specific definition to kingdom life. It is dictated by the very nature of God and His King, Christ, whose character will fill eternity. Since we will be perfected and made like Him, the environment of eternity will reflect a consistent culture through our lives as citizens of the eternal nation of God. As kingdom people it is our privilege to learn the culture of heaven and begin to live it out here, reflecting the eternal culture of our ultimate home.

As we have learned, Scripture is clear that we are already citizens of heaven (Phil. 3:20) and that our behavior, attitudes, and responses to life should reflect that citizenship. If you travel to other countries, you are readily aware that each culture has its distinctive patterns of life. Europeans pile their food on their forks upside down. While it seems that the scoop side of the fork is the better place to hold food, for some reason they like their food stacked on the back. It's an evident mark of someone from Europe. Asians show deep respect and deference that most westerners cannot understand. Their culture flows through strict social rules that relate to place in the family, class, and status in the marketplace.

Meanwhile in the sub-Sahara of Africa, the larger a woman is, the more beautiful she is thought to be. Men have status in the community based on the size of their wives. If you are wealthy you have plenty of money to feed your family, and the largeness of your wives reflects your wealth.

Even here in the States we reflect differences in taste, style, and accent depending on where we were raised and to which group we belong. Likewise, the kingdom of Christ has a distinct culture, and as citizens of heaven we are called to demonstrate the marvelous habits of heaven in the midst of a culture fallen in despair and disgrace.

HOW WOULD YOU KNOW?

How would you recognize a kingdom person if you were looking for one? Watch for someone whose sense of significance is settled and who stands secure regardless of his circumstances. Look for a life that has hope in times when others would despair. Watch for signs of an unflinching allegiance to a holy God who is above and beyond. Look for one whose life is characterized by conquest over the adversary and conformity to the unique culture of the kingdom. The homeward-bent pilgrim basks in the privileges of belonging to the kingdom and faithfully fulfills his responsibilities to the King.

What specifically are the principles and practices that are unique to kingdom behavior?

CHAPTER THIRTEEN

KINGDOM CHARACTER

RIGHTEOUSNESS REIGNS

ony Evans, founder of The Urban Alternative and pastor of Oak Cliff Bible Fellowship in Dallas, when speaking about the impact of eternity on our lives, says that God intends our lives to be like "sneak previews of the really big show to come." Unfortunately, many of us are so consumed by the passing show of this present world that we rarely give others a glimpse of what life will be like in the kingdom of eternity to which we belong.

Even unbelievers expect glimpses of eternity from our lives. Obviously, they wouldn't put it that way, but they expect to see a difference. The authentic difference is defined by the kingdom identity that we have in Christ. When it is permitted to preoccupy our minds, hearts, and self-awareness, it reflects a distinctive lifestyle that cannot be ignored by a watching world.

If you've traveled much by car you've noticed how anxious people are to announce where they're headed, particularly if it is special. Recently I noticed a car with California plates manuevering through Chicago rush-hour traffic. As I pulled alongside I noticed that it was packed to the brim with clothes and boxes, with two co-eds in the front seat—one sipping a bottle of juice and the other navigating. Across the back window a sign announced "California or Bust." After a long year in college they were proudly heading home.

KINGDOM ATTIRE

Boarding a Tampa-bound jet one Saturday, I noticed that most of the passengers were on their way to the Chicago Bears game against the Bucs. Their destination was obvious. They walked on to the plane decked in Bears scarves, hats, sweaters, and sweatshirts.

Our kingdom behavior is a clear announcement that we are headed toward heaven.

Displaying the culture of eternity is like those few people that all of us know who are ahead of the fashion trends. Long before we are wearing sideburns they are growing theirs. Their tie and lapel widths are clear announcements of fashions to come. I've never been to a fashion show, but on occasion I've watched them on TV. Famous designers display their new fashions on specially selected models who saunter down the runway for all to see what the future will look like. This is all done to the glory and credit of the designer who makes the final appearance down the runway with the models clustered around to the applause of the crowd.

As kingdom travelers, if we are doing it right, our lives are clear and compelling statements of our destiny; announcements of the eternal lifestyle to come. And we wear the conduct of the kingdom to which we belong—to the glory of our King who is the designer of its culture. In the end we too will gather around Him dressed in His righteousness and appear with Him when "at the name of Jesus every knee should bow, of those who are in heaven, and on earth, and under the earth, and that every tongue should confess that Jesus Christ is Lord, to the glory of God the Father" (Phil. 2:10–11).

I don't know of a worse feeling socially than to show up at some great shindig seriously underdressed. Think of not knowing it was a black-tie affair and arriving in a sweater and slacks.

It would be particularly painful if you were sent there to represent your boss or company.

Kingdom travelers are God's carefully chosen persons to display His dramatically different designer wardrobe to a world that is curious about who we are and what we claim to be. We travel here as representatives of His kingdom and as such should proudly display a life consistent with the kingdom's culture.

REPRESENTING THE KING

Unfortunately, because we are unwilling to let Christ reign in our lives, we often embarrass the reputation of the King with our soiled garments that reflect the patterns of life in this present world. Of the many embarrassing things that have happened in my life, few measure with the trip I took to represent Moody Bible Institute to major donors who were considering a large gift that would allow us to proceed with a strategic building project for our campus. I was relatively new in my job, and this would be my first opportunity to meet these generous partners as president of the Institute. Dr. Sweeting, my predecessor, had often met with them, and on this occasion he and I were both going to see if we could secure a commitment to this project and also to introduce me to them as the new president of MBI. Dr. Sweeting would be going on to another city. For me it was a one-day trip, out in the morning, back in the evening. That meant that I had brought no change of clothes.

About a half hour into the flight, I suddenly felt a burning sensation on my lap which signaled that something had gone dreadfully wrong. One glance confirmed my worst fears. I had spilled my entire cup of coffee and was now sitting in a puddle of Colombia's best. I was soaked from the front of my white dress shirt down my suit to my knees. I excused myself and walked toward the rest room to see what remedial work could be done. My embarrassment turned to despair as I thought about the fact that this was my first opportunity to represent Moody to these folks. As I looked in the mirror, my worst fears were confirmed. A flight attendant kindly brought me the last can of club soda that they had, which she said would be my only hope to clean the coffee from my clothes.

It probably goes without saying that I had to disrobe and start the cleaning process from the inside out.

Dr. Sweeting knocked on the door about halfway through the process and mentioned that the flight attendant had told him about another gentleman who had a similar experience. They had hung his clothes up in front of an air vent to dry and cut a hole in a blanket to put over him as he sat in his seat waiting to redress. I chose instead to work out my own drying procedure in the claustrophobic confines of that washroom. An hour and forty-five minutes later, I began to feel my ears pop and knew we were making our descent. I had been marginally successful with my suit pants, but my shirt was hopelessly stained. I went back out to my seat, to the gazes of the other passengers, and as we landed I must admit I felt less than good about showing up in this condition.

By redemption and the grace of God, we have been cleansed and clothed in the righteousness of God through the finished work of Jesus Christ. This is the only way that we can stand in His presence. Unfortunately, we tend to inflict damage to our redemptive wardrobe by spotting and staining our lives with the destructive, polluting impurities of this present world. This may be exactly what James had in mind when he wrote, "This is pure and undefiled religion in the sight of our God and Father, to visit orphans and widows in their distress, and to keep oneself unstained by the world" (1:27).

What then is the appropriate lifestyle with which to announce to a watching world our kingdom identity? If we are to live in light of the world to come by managing our world within under the authority of the King, it is important to recognize that the culture and characteristics of this eternal kingdom are molded, managed, and defined by the characteristics of Christ. His awesome, all-consuming presence by the nature of His compelling purity and power shapes the character, protocol, and culture of His kingdom.

In seminary certain students' majors became obvious by the particular characteristics they reflected as a result of their admiration for their major professor: a gesture, a facial response, the repetition of an unusual phrase or word that they had sometimes unconsciously adopted. So struck with admiration for their mentor, their mentor's characteristics became assimilated into their life. To this day I have a friend who some twenty-five years later is a carbon copy of his theology professor.

So it is with our relationship to Christ. The power of His character—in fact, the complete rightness of all that He is—consumes the culture of the kingdom. And those of us who admire Him assimilate the customs of the King into our lives. Isn't that the call of the Spirit in our lives, to be like Christ? It is the measure of our maturity and the mark of the kingdom (Eph. 3:13–15).

What would the culture of the kingdom look like exposed in the realm of our existence?

RIGHTEOUSNESS REIGNS

The central tenet of the culture of His kingdom is *righteousness.* Everything in the kingdom is measured by this standard. As the book of Hebrews claims of the King, "But of the Son He says, 'Thy throne, O God, is forever and ever, and the righteous scepter is the scepter of His kingdom. Thou hast loved righteousness and hated lawlessness; therefore God, Thy God, hath anointed Thee with the oil of gladness above Thy companions'" (1:8–9). Righteousness is God's absolute standard of what is correct. It is the standard by which all conduct is and will be measured. In a graphic illustration of the essence of righteousness, Israel is warned not to use *unrighteous* weights in the marketplace. Unrighteous weights didn't measure to the correct standard and thus could be used to cheat the customer. Righteousness is related not to the standards of our politically correct world, but rather to God who is and who defines the standard.

All of our responses to life, whether social, economic, emotive, sensual, or material, are measured by His correct character and nature. This means we can be unrighteous by both being more strict than God, as were the Pharisees, or more tolerant than God. Strictness is not next to godliness if it is more strict than He, and liberty is not freedom in Christ if it is a license to leave the righteous center of God. Paul underscores this when he defines the protocol of kingdom behavior not being comprised of "eating and drinking" (i.e., earth-side material and physical activities) but rather, "righteousness and peace and joy in the Holy Spirit" (Rom. 14:17). The context of this statement by Paul is of great importance to those of us who are committed to this first-wave expression of kingdom culture.

RIGHTEOUS RELATIONSHIPS

Paul indicates that kingdom living here and now directly impacts the quality of our relationships. That's why he wraps the centerpiece of righteousness with peace and joy. He is writing to a divided church in Rome where believers who felt at liberty to eat meat offered to idols were offending—in fact, damaging—the lives of brothers who because of past associations with idolatry were stumbling spiritually by this practice. Paul appeals to the kind of kingdom living that is governed by the *righteous* law of love (v. 15) which elevates the needs of a brother over personal desires and encourages them to follow a path of behavior that will promote peace and joy in the community of belief. Kingdom living relates to whether or not our lives are governed by what is right before God. In this case, putting the needs of others before our own desires (i.e., eating and drinking), just as Christ the King put our needs before His desires. It should not go unnoticed that eternity will be marked by peace and joy. The community of the King should be marked by these eternal commodities. Our righteous love for one another is the impetus for blessing our environment with the presence of peace and joy.

DRESSING FOR THE BIG EVENT

Not only does righteousness impact our relationships in the body of Christ; it has a direct impact on eternity as well, particularly the marriage supper of the Lamb. John, in the book of Revelation, recorded a dramatic wedding picture that relates to the kingdom characteristic of righteousness defining and characterizing our lives. When the church, the bride of Christ, is received by Christ, the Bridegroom, His bride (the church) will be clothed in the finest linen—both bright and clean. This wedding dress, the text goes on to say, is comprised of the "righteous acts of the saints." John wrote:

> Let us rejoice and be glad and give glory to Him, for the marriage of the Lamb has come and His bride has made herself ready.

And it was given to her to clothe herself in fine linen, bright and clean; for the fine linen is the righteous acts of the saints. And he said to me, "Write, 'Blessed are those who are invited to the marriage supper of the Lamb.'" And He said to me, "These are true words of God." (Rev. 19:7–9)

I like to think that on my pilgrimage toward paradise, the righteous acts of my life are weaving threads into the beautiful gown that the church will wear on that grand and glorious day. As Paul noted in Eph. 5:25–27, Christ "loved the church and gave Himself up for her; that He might sanctify her, having cleansed her by the washing of water with the word, that He might present to Himself the church in all her glory, having no spot or wrinkle or any such thing; but that she should be holy and blameless."

I'll never forget what life was like in the months and weeks preceding our only daughter's wedding. There were long lists of things to do and details to be covered. Preeminent on the list was picking out Libby's dress. What she would wear on that day would adorn her beauty and grace. It was obviously important to Libby that her dress be appropriately tailored to enhance her stature. But most importantly, Libby wanted to make sure that Rod, her soon-to-be husband, would be pleased with how she looked in the dress. That seemed to be more important than what anyone else thought about the dress. And so it will be with us on that day when we, His bride, present ourselves to Christ, the Bridegroom, the lover of our souls. The only fitting way to present ourselves and to bring pleasure to Him will be to wear the resplendent beauty of the righteous acts of our lives.

Our righteousness here is an investment in the glory of the world to come. Though this present world scorns a life of righteousness and tells us that we are good for nothing, the truth is that we are righteous for a very good reason. We are not good because we have to be or because we might get caught and embarrassed if we aren't. Righteousness is not embraced to avoid the consequences of unrighteousness in this present world. Righteousness is expressed because it is the very fabric of the kingdom and the glory of Christ. We wear it without shame, humbly, to the glory of the Designer, and to express the very nature of the eternity to which we belong. When righteousness is embraced for reasons like these, it is no longer a burden but a privileged blessing.

Kingdom travelers also understand that this present world seductively crafts its own systems of correctness that often contradict the righteous standard of the King. Kingdom persons reject politically correct standards for the standard that is both true and eternal. We choose to live by the standard of the King who will finally judge all of us. To be judged by this world's system of conduct and found wanting is insignificant by comparison.

CHAPTER FOURTEEN

THE KINGDOM LOOK

ETERNAL VIRTUES ABOVE
EARTH-SIDE VALUES

George Sweeting served as the sixth president of Moody for sixteen distinguished years. Needless to say, it was a challenge for me to follow his season of service at Moody. Not only had he been an outstanding leader, but he looked liked the quintessential president. His wavy white hair, soft eyes, and sensitive yet determined countenance made him look like the consummate president. His pulpit mannerisms were impeccable; his representation of Moody without stain. One of the broadcasting people at Moody said to me that Dr. Sweeting never gave them any reason to be ashamed. Simply put, he not only had the look; he had the character to support and advance the cause to which Christ had called him.

It's like that for those of us who are called to manage the world within in such a way that we express to a watching world an accurate statement of both the look and the character of the kingdom. As we think of reflecting the righteousness that is the core of the kingdom, we need to know what this righteousness specifically looks like as it is lived out. What actual biblical targets can we focus on? What mirrors can we hang in the closet of our souls to check the kingdom look that God has designed?

Obviously, a righteous life will reflect the compelling qualities of the fruit of the Spirit. Gal. 5:22–23 lists the kingdom fashions that adorn a pilgrim who is committed to righteousness. We can't miss the fact that the qualities of love, joy, peace, patience, kindness, goodness, faithfulness, gentleness, and self-control are *fruits.* They are the result of a process that involves our walking in (submitting to) the Spirit of the King who always leads us to righteous behavior, the centerpiece of kingdom protocol.

Interestingly, in Galatians Paul contrasts these kingdom marks against the domain of darkness from which we have been delivered. The fashions of a fading, past, conquered, degenerating kingdom are: "immorality, impurity, sensuality, idolatry, sorcery, enmities, strife, jealousy, outbursts of anger, disputes, dissensions, factions, envying, drunkenness, carousing, and things like these" (Gal. 5:19–21). Even if there were no world beyond and no kingdom within, there would hardly be any contest between which qualities of life would be more desirable.

What then are the elements of righteousness that cultivate and produce these kingdom fruits in our lives? Since *righteousness* is such a huge word covering the waterfront of all that is right before God according to His standards, we can categorize it into three segments: righteous *principles* and righteous *perspectives* that lead to righteous *practices.* We will look at the perspectives and practices in the following chapter.

KINGDOM VIRTUES

First, in this chapter let's explore the compelling principles of the kingdom. When we are driven by these principles, they inevitably produce the kingdom image in our lives. In fact, these principles are in reality more than just "values." They constitute God's moral authority in our lives, and as such they are the *virtues* that define and dictate kingdom living.

Interestingly, we hear little about "virtue" in this present world. All of our talk about principles that determine behavior is in terms of "values." There is a reason. Since this present domain rejects the thought of absolutes there is no longer a supreme, single moral authority. Earthbound persons are free to structure their own set of values. One person's set of values is as valid as another's. Therefore, nothing is really virtuous since virtue smacks of that which is best, that which is morally superior. In a very real sense this present world has lost its virtue because it has rejected Christ the King as absolute and final moral authority.

Stephen Covey in his book *First Things First* says of the weakness of values:

> To value something is to esteem it to be of worth. And values are critically important. Our values drive our choices and actions. But we can value many different things—love, security, a big house, money in the bank, status, recognition, fame. Just because we value something does not necessarily mean it will create quality-of-life results. When what we value is in opposition to the natural laws that govern peace of mind and quality of life, we base our lives on illusion and set ourselves up for failure. We cannot be a law unto ourselves.[1]

Speaking of the importance of principled virtues he concludes, "Values will *not* bring quality-of-life results . . . *unless we value principles.*"[2]

William Bennett, former U.S. Secretary of Health, Education and Welfare, compiled *The Book of Virtues* in an effort to re-inculcate the notion of virtue into our society. In this best-seller he noted the difference between values and virtues. He wrote, "Today we speak about values, and how important it is for us to 'have them' as if they were beads on a string or marbles in a pouch." He goes on to say in contrast that virtues are not something to be possessed but "something to be, the most important thing to be."[3]

Historian Gertrude Himmelfarb adds that "the shift from 'virtue' to 'values' has had other unfortunate consequences," including confining the idea of virtue to the idea of "chastity and marital fidelity," while forgetting to emphasize "the classical virtues of wisdom, justice, temperance, and courage, or the Christian ones of faith, hope, and charity."[4]

When Bennett's book on virtues first came out I went to my local bookstore to acquire a copy. After leafing through it I took it to the counter where a trendy, bookish-type clerk took my money. As he did I naively said, "This looks like it could be a best-seller"—to which he replied rather caustically, "I hope not." I was puzzled until I realized that the thought of virtues, moral absolutes that define character and behavior, are not only foreign in this present world but unwelcome as well.

As kingdom transients, we commit ourselves to the moral absolutes of the King and strive to emulate these virtues in the midst of varying and often conflicting values in the world around us. The kingdom mind-set elevates eternal virtues as the highest point of success, admiration, and personal affirmation. Significantly, kingdom virtues feature character above credentials. In the community of belief, respectability and honor are grounded in character rather than position, power, or wealth. The poorest, least credentialed of us who is a virtuous kingdom traveler will find honor in our midst.

Unfortunately, many of us have opted for honor in the earthside values of fame, fortune, and wealth. For some of us, power is assumed to be in position rather than purity. Performance eclipses piety. Yet, embracing the principles, the virtues, of the kingdom as the noblest element of our pilgrimage focuses our passion on kingdom character rather than earthbound stature.

What then are the virtues that produce kingdom righteousness? Since it is the righteousness of Christ that shapes the codes and conduct of the kingdom, we need to look to the principles, the virtues that Christ embraced in the defining moments of His life. In fact, the Incarnation, God in our form in the person of Christ, demonstrated for us what the King would do if He were on earth. That, in turn, demonstrates for us the essence of kingdom behavior. Christ is the visible link to the character and quality of eternity in human earth-side dynamics. The moral authority that He imposed on His own person and relationships casts a clear vision of the virtues to which we must aspire as kingdom travelers.

DEFINING VIRTUES

There are at least seven kingdom virtues reflected in Christ's life. They are best understood in contrast to the earthbound value with which they compete. They are: *truth*, as opposed to tolerance; *grace*, rather than greed; *love*, rather than self-centeredness; *servanthood*, in contrast to significance; *self-control*, as opposed to sensualism; *justice*, instead of oppression; *humility*, as opposed to haughtiness. These seven virtues, when embraced, forge kingdom character that gives our lives a compelling uniqueness. Let's school ourselves in Christ's kingdom responses in this present world.

1. Truth

There is little doubt that the ruling value of this present, passing world is tolerance. Since society has no moral authority that dictates the absolutes to which it should strive, everything is legitimate as long as it doesn't harm or hinder another person. Because in their enlightenment earthbound philosophers have come to believe that there is no real right and wrong, to be truly modern we must tolerate everything. This is why gay liberation, abortion, sexual expression without limits, and other sinful activities are fully tolerated. This is why varieties of secular philosophies can be hailed as valid even in the face of their debilitating outcomes, and this is why we are told to seek the truth but are punished when we say we have found it.

Yet, kingdom persons find their lives formed by the virtue of truth. This inevitably puts us in conflict with the domain from which we have been delivered. Truth by its very nature is intolerant. If there is truth, then there is error. If there is right, then there is wrong. A kingdom person who is committed to truth will always tolerate those who are in error but will never tolerate error itself. Yet, of all the principles of righteousness, truth must reign supreme. It is not that we arrogantly and arbitrarily claim to know truth; it is rather that we are people of the King who by His very nature is true. In fact, the penetrating impression that Christ made while on earth was that He was full of truth (John 1:14) and that His truth was the reflected glory of His Father.

As kingdom people we both embrace and express truth. The source of truth is the authoritative Word of God and as such gives us solid life-related conclusions that are true regardless of the state of denial our present culture is in. We are people who speak the truth in love and confidence. We are true to our word and commitments. We are true to who we say we are and what we claim to be. We refuse to lie, deceive, cheat, or in any way erode what is true by either action or attitude. The character we develop as people of the truth is marked by integrity, reliability, and transparency. As people of the truth we are committed to what is truly fair and just. As such we become champions for the oppressed and helpers of those who are genuine victims. Most of all, we are true to God in word, deed, thought, and attitude.

God is true. All that He says and does is true. You can count on that. He is true to Himself, His Word, His people, His promises, and the entirety of His character. In His rule there is no error, no hypocrisy, no unfaithfulness, no injustice, no deceit. As such, His kingdom is characterized by truth—a virtue toward which kingdom persons strive.

2. Grace

Standing alongside this certain and immovable virtue of truth is the second virtue that was clearly evident in the King: grace. When the apostle John remembered his life with the King, he remarked that Christ was full of grace (1 John 1:14). Truth is final and firm, while grace enables and encourages the struggler to come to his or her full potential in the truth. It enables us to recover when we fall. The domain of Satan celebrates those who have the power to personally advance themselves regardless of how ruthless they are with others. Grace focuses our power on the empowerment and enablement of others to overcome and succeed. Grace is the perfect complement to truth. It paves the way to living by the standard of truth.

In this present world the weak are victimized, discarded, and marginalized. In the kingdom, grace encourages and enables the weak in our midst. It is even extended to our enemies. Grace forgives, enabling restoration. Grace shares resources to meet needs. Grace patiently mentors. Grace listens, understands, and loves. Grace goes into danger first. Grace sees potential rather than problems.

Where would we be today if our lives had not been sustained by the grace of the King who shares His power and resources with us for our eternal benefit? His amazing grace is a kingdom virtue. An eternal fashion that will benefit all who come within its reach.

When the Pharisees brought the adulterous woman to Jesus, she had obviously been framed to set up a situation in which they could publicly discredit Christ. Christ said nothing to the Pharisees; He simply wrote something twice in the sand. There is little doubt that His finger writing in the sand was meant to reflect the God of Israel who, because of His grace toward Israel who had sinned against Him, wrote the tablets of the law twice. To the Pharisees it was a reminder of the God of grace, and to the woman He extended both grace and truth: "Go, and sin no more" (John 8:11 KJV).

The Nations Ford Baptist Church in Charlotte, North Carolina, found just the right place to plant their church where they could develop a ministry for God's glory. It was a vacant church building on the edge of what had been a long-standing blue-collar, white area of town. In fact, the Grand Wizard of the Ku Klux Klan lived down the street, as did many adherents of his sect. Needless to say the prospect of them settling into this neighborhood met stiff resistance in the community, given the fact that the Nations Ford Baptist Church is a body of African-American believers. The pastor, Phil Davis, could have led his church down the road of political conquest by using the ACLU to guarantee their place there. He could have opted to call the editor of the *Charlotte Observer* to bring to bear the power of the media to publicly intimidate the neighborhood resistance. If the Nations Ford church wanted a still stronger power play, Davis and church members could have called the Advocacy Hotline at the U.S. Justice Department and retained a federal civil rights lawyer to protect their rights. Or they could have decided that this was simply another case of the racism that historically subjugated our nation and retreated into a cocoon of deepening self-pity and bitterness toward their enemies who surrounded them in the neighborhood.

Instead, Nations Ford Baptist Church did something far more dramatic and effective. They reflected their commitment to the lordship of Christ.

Members of the Nations Ford Baptist Church understood that there was another option available to them, one grounded in

God's plan for penetrating hostile environments with the good news of Jesus Christ. Realizing that the neighborhood around their new property was struggling with encroaching poverty and unemployment and that many of the residents were being litigated by creditors, the church focused its attention on a ministry of compassion to the needs of the neighborhood. Since some of the members of the congregation were legal, financial, and medical professionals, they opened an office outside the community (to avoid causing embarrassment to their new neighbors for coming to these services) and began to give legal, medical, and financial counsel and service to their new neighbors. The business persons in the church offered employment opportunities to the unemployed, and over a brief period of time these acts of grace toward their enemies melted the resistance and opened the doors of that community, not only to the Nations Ford Baptist Church but to the gospel of Jesus Christ.

Since 1988, the church has grown from 11 to 1,200 members. Most significant is that 70 percent of this church growth is made up of new believers. Nations Ford Baptist also has started two mission churches. It was the power of grace in the midst of a hostile neighborhood that melted the resistance and opened hearts to the power of redemption.

Phil Davis and his church are clearly kingdom travelers. When they extended marvelous grace to the community, they forecast the dawning of a day, of an eternity where grace abounds and the indebted will sing:

> Marvelous grace of our loving Lord
>> Grace that exceeds our sin and our guilt
> Yonder on Calvary's mount outpoured
>> There where the blood of the Lamb was spilt.
> Grace, grace, God's grace—
>> grace that will pardon and cleanse within!
> Grace, grace, God's grace,
>> grace that is greater than all our sin.

3. Love

Fewer virtues find as much support in the everyday activities of Christ as the obvious expression of His unconditional love. Toward all! His love transcended ethnic, gender, moral, socioeconomic barriers. Jesus loved tax collectors and sinners. Wealthy and poor. Pharisees and prostitutes. And He loved not by choice or random decision. He is love. He can't help but love. It is an essential aspect of His character. What then is the definition of this kingdom virtue?

The kingdom principle of love requires that we choose (whether we feel good about it or not, whether we like the person who is to be loved or not, whether he deserves it or not) to reach out and yield ourselves and our resources to the needs of others. As Christ commanded, we are first to love Him (yield completely to Him) and then, because we are yielded to Him, follow His command to love our neighbor as ourselves. In fact, this sequence (Matt. 22:34–40) indicates that we can tell how much we love God by the way we treat those around us.

The competing cultural value is not hate but self-centeredness. In this "look out for number one" world where self-interest to the disregard of others' needs is encouraged, the authentic pilgrim denies the earth-side grip of self and seeks to be a blessing to others.

The pressure to claim and cling to our rights may be the greatest challenge of all to transcend; to demand privileges and personal attention. But kingdom protocol elevates love as a distinct virtue. And, in a world where self-centeredness has isolated us into ghettos of one; where our self-centeredness has left us lonely and unfulfilled; where hearts are starved for true love and concern with no strings attached; the impact of love flowing from a kingdom life will cut like a laser beam through the darkness in this present world and enter lives that are looking for the light of Christ the King.

Love as a kingdom ethic is to be focused toward God and neighbor and more specifically to fellow followers of Christ (John 13:34–34); husbands to wives (Eph. 5:25); toward the flock in feeding and caring ministries (John 21:15–17); and even toward our enemies (Matt. 5:43–48).

Buster Soaries, pastor of First Baptist Church of Lincoln Gardens in Sommerset, New York, has a clear commitment in expressing kingdom love, even to his enemies. Several years ago he was kidnapped by five drug dealers whose plan was to take his life. With a shotgun in his face, a .45 at the back of his head, and a rifle jammed in his side, Buster was chauffered to a vacant lot and dragged out of the car early one morning. Just before the guns were fired, the driver noticed a police car parked on a nearby highway. Fearing that the shots would be heard, they threw Buster back into the car. Nearly five hours later, their plans foiled, the kidnappers were instructed by their gang lord to let Buster go. They made it clear to him that they would get him later.

Talk about enemies! Buster had every reason to both fear and hate those men. Not yet a believer, he had resolved to take revenge next time he saw them. It was an understandable response . . . that is, until he later encountered Christ and began learning what it meant to live by the unique principles of the kingdom.

Some time later, at a gathering of more than 20,000 at Madison Square Garden, to Buster's surprise the man who had once held a .45 to the back of his head was standing in front of him. Immediately, a surge of hatred and retaliation flowed within him, alongside the Spirit's clear reminder that he needed to demonstrate the principles of the kingdom by loving his enemy. Would he seek to protect himself and shy away out of fear? Would he seek to remediate the injustice of the past and use this as an opportunity to even the score? Or would he discard those earth-side responses in order to use the moment to model the love of Christ?

Buster approached his "enemy" and, much to the kidnapper's shock, hugged him, told him he loved him, and said that if he needed anything to let him know; he would be happy to help him in any way. Buster says, "That man almost dropped dead right then and there."

And the King rejoiced that through the faithfulness of His servant, His love had cut like a laser beam from the stretches of eternity into the darkness of that man's heart.

4. Servanthood

The fourth virtue that shapes our conduct as kingdom travelers is servanthood. It is a fascinating twist to note that when Christ the King arrived on our planet, having the highest position in the universe, He used His position to serve. In fact, He perceived his identity to be that of a servant. Struggling with the domain's obsession with significance, the King focused His ministry on enabling His disciples to take on the perspective of a servant. They were much more prone to sit around discussing who would hold the highest office of significance and power in the kingdom. In a dramatic and instructive moment, the King put on a towel and washed their feet to demonstrate the importance of servanthood. In fact, He said to them in another context where greatness was clearly the goal of all twelve disciples, "You know that the rulers of the Gentiles lord it over them, and their great men exercise authority over them. It is not so among you, but whoever wishes to become great among you shall be your servant, and whoever wishes to be first among you shall be your slave; just as the Son of Man did not come to be served, but to serve, and to give His life a ransom for many" (Matt. 20:25–28).

Paul points to the King as our example where He commands that we

> Do nothing from selfishness or empty conceit, but with humility of mind let each of you regard one another as more important than himself; do not merely look out for your own personal interests, but also for the interests of others. Have this attitude in yourselves which was also in Christ Jesus, who, although He existed in the form of God, did not regard equality with God a thing to be grasped, but emptied Himself, taking the form of a bond-servant, and being made in the likeness of men. And being found in appearance as a man, He humbled Himself by becoming obedient to the point of death, even death on a cross. (Phil. 2:3–8)

Success in the kingdom is measured in our service to others. The final divine compliment will be reserved only for those travelers who are "good and faithful servants" as they travel toward home (Matt. 25:21).

The Promise Keepers movement, mass gatherings of men to worship and commit themselves to basic biblical principles, has been so successful that it has drawn the attention of the secular press. A recent television documentary covered the waterfront of Promise Keepers, with segments of gay rights activists, abortion proponents, and representatives of the more fanatical fringe of the women's liberation movement citing their displeasure and disagreements with what they suppose Promise Keepers to be. It is clear that the kingdom commitments of Promise Keepers to loving God and growing strong families fly in the face of the values of this present world. At the close of the documentary, they interviewed a man who was an avowed Promise Keeper. They showed him in his home with his wife and children. He said at the close of his comments that, while he was a leader in his family, he was a servant to his wife.

The news anchors, in their wrap-up discussion of the documentary, commented on that statement. One of them said, "I thought that was very interesting that he said he was the servant of his wife. Isn't it an anomaly that one could be a leader and a servant?"

Well, it is . . . if all you have is the mind-set of this present world. But if you know Christ, then you know that that's exactly who He was. And it's what He calls us to be as well. The Promise Keeper in that interview adorned his life with the likeness of His King.

5. Self-Control

As we will note later, this world's most powerful urges flow from the passions of our souls: the lust of the flesh, the lust of our eyes, and the pride of life (1 John 2:16). All of these have to do with the seductive power of our senses. We are built to be sensual in the right sense. In fact, if we didn't have these sensual capacities, we wouldn't want to eat, procreate, succeed in our work, or relate well to others. A life without these impulses would be a life of vegetation.

The problem with our senses is not that we have them, it is that this world's system encourages us to use them solely for our own pleasure and gain, regardless of the righteous context in which they are intended to be enjoyed. Kingdom people are not controlled by their sensual urges but bring them under the control of the King who guides them to productive ends for His glory and the gain of the kingdom. And as a bonus, we find fulfillment and joy in our sensual experiences without the guilt and destructive erosion that takes place in our soul when we spend our passions on ourselves.

Nowhere does the King more dramatically demonstrate this kingdom virtue of self-control then when He came face-to-face with the king of this domain of darkness in the wilderness when his basic sensual instincts were most vulnerable (Matt. 4:1–11). After He had fasted for forty days, Satan lured Him to satisfy Himself by following the adversary's promptings. Satan tempted Him with food, self-authentication, power, fame, and position. Yet Christ put Himself under a higher moral authority than Satan, used the power of the Word of God to direct His responses, and, as a result, said no to His impulses so that He could say yes to the honor and glory of His Father.

The issue for those of us who occupy His kingdom is under whose moral authority do we live? And to whom will we be loyal regardless of the inner impulses? Will it be the prince of this planet, our own inner urges, or the clear Word of God which directs and protects us as we travel toward home?

The virtue of self-control stands as a clear kingdom mark in the face of the phenomenal pressure of the sensualism of our day. Our senses are seduced to be spent on themselves at every turn. Yet kingdom travelers place their senses under the Spirit's control through the moral authority of the righteous directives of the Word of God. Interestingly, as Christ resisted the seductive impulses of His senses He became our High Priest, able to understand and empathize with us as we are tempted. As such, He readily gives us grace (His power and enablement) to guarantee our success as well (Heb. 4:14–16). When we yield our urgings to His control, our character assumes an obvious purity, both internally and externally, that is a unique display of kingdom righteousness.

Control is the key concept. This present world encourages us to stay personally in control of relationships, destiny, wealth, power, and passion. Virtue states the issue is not what we control but who or what controls us. If it is our senses and environment, then we are earthlings at heart. If it is the Word and His Spirit, then we are authentic kingdom adherents.

6. Justice

Justice is the sixth kingdom virtue. Kingdom justice stands in sharp contrast to the blatant and prevalent oppression and treachery toward which permanent residents on this planet are so prone. If all that we have is this world and what we can get and gain here, then we'll do whatever we can to advance and empower ourselves even if it is at the expense of others. As a result the weaker, less fortunate elements of society become pawns to be used and discarded for personal gain.

These oppressive tendencies are denounced throughout Scripture. In fact, God distanced Himself from Israel who, though faithful in terms of their ritual practices, had failed to justly deal with oppressive behavior. In Isaiah chapter 58 Israel pleads for a greater sense of His presence and power, and God responds:

> Is this not the fast which I chose, to loosen the bonds of wickedness, to undo the bands of the yoke, and to let the oppressed go free, and break every yoke? Is it not to divide your bread with the hungry, and bring the homeless poor into the house; when you see the naked, to cover him; and not to hide yourself from your own flesh? Then your light will break out like the dawn, and your recovery will speedily spring forth; and your righteousness will go before you; the glory of the Lord will be your rear guard. Then you will call, and the Lord will answer; you will cry, and He will say, "Here I am." If you remove the yoke from your midst, the pointing of the finger, and speaking wickedness, and if you give yourself to the hungry, and satisfy the desire of the afflicted, then your light will rise in darkness, and your gloom will become like midday. And the Lord will continually guide you, and satisfy your desire in scorched places, and give strength to your bones; and you will be like a watered garden, and like a spring of water whose waters do not fail. (Isa. 58:6–11)

It is interesting how quiet we are, as kingdom believers, about oppression and the oppressive systems of this present world. Few voices are raised against racist structures that intentionally deny empowerment, worth, and dignity to gifted and precious persons because of passport or pigment. We raise our voices against pornography and prostitution because we see them as problems of sexual perversion when we should be equally concerned about the use, abuse, and destruction of women and children who are oppressively used within the system to empower and prosper those who control them. Pimps and pornographers brutalize the weak and vulnerable in our midst for their own gain. Child abuse—whether sexual, physical, mental, or emotional—is a heinous expression of the powerful oppressing the weak. The problem of drugs is bigger than its threat to our own children and the moral fabric of society. It is sold and traded in a system that controls and oppressively manipulates weaker people in society. Slavery was a blatant expression of injustice to people of worth and dignity. Apartheid is an injustice in this present world. Ethnic cleansing is a violation of the just rights of humanity.

Four decades ago an African-American Christian woman in her forties refused to surrender her seat to a white man on a bus in Montgomery, Alabama. Many now call Rosa Parks the mother of the civil rights movement and call her act one of courage. But Rosa calls her action one of faith.

"I felt the Lord would give me strength to endure whatever I had to face," Rosa said recently. "It was time for someone to stand up—or, in my case, to sit down. I refused to move."[5]

Kingdom people must be willing to stand, or sit, for what is right and just. We will not oppress, control, or prey on the weaker ones around us for our own gain. In fact, kingdom grace seeks to protect and empower them. Not only are we just in all our dealings with others; we cry out against injustice and seek to loosen the bonds of wickedness . . . and to let the oppressed go free . . . to divide our bread with the hungry.

While Christ our King often raised the standard of justice against oppression, nowhere is it more dramatic than when He cleansed the Temple (Mark 11:15–17). Many have thought that the offense was selling things in the Temple (and as a result some have concluded we should never sell things at church, certainly not on Sunday). It actually refers to the selling of animals and the changing of currency that was carried on as a service to pilgrims who had come from far countries and as such were not able to bring sacrificial animals with them to the Temple. The offense was that the money changers and those who marketed sacrifices were charging exorbitant rates to helpless pilgrims who had no choice but to buy their sacrifices. They were running an oppressive economic enterprise. In order to buy a dove you had to change your money for Temple currency at unjust rates and then pay several times market value for your sacrifice. And the text indicates that the religious leaders of the day were all part of the scheme. That's why Christ called the merchants thieves and robbers. They were unjustly charging helpless pilgrims for their own gain.

There is no scam more blatantly unjust than a scheme that plays on a person's instincts to please and serve God. That is what makes religious charlatans and immoral religious leaders so much more detestable than other thieves or womanizers. Their victims are lured into their schemes within an environment that should protect and enable. As Christ said, "Is it not written, 'My house shall be called a house of prayer for all the nations'? But you have made it a robbers' den" (Mark 11:17). Injustice in the name of a just God is a serious offense to the kingdom.

The King became our champion all the way to the cross when we were oppressed in sin and hopelessly doomed by the treachery of this present dark domain. The cross stands as a symbol of justice where the price of sin was paid and the oppressed were set eternally free. Justice stands at the heart of the righteousness of His kingdom. It is guided by truth, empowered by grace, motivated by love, activated by a servant's heart, and governed by the control of the Spirit. It is the culmination of kingdom virtues. All of them come together at the cross.

Few have exemplified justice in action on behalf of God more than William Wilberforce. As a young man, he rose in British politics and became one of the youngest people to ever hold a seat in Parliament. Though slight of build and somewhat anemic in appearance, his oratory and rhetoric powerfully moved the British populace. He became a dear friend of Pitt, the prime minister, and word on the street was that he would himself someday be prime minister of Britain.

His heart, however, was troubled by the fact that Britain had become one of the leading slave-trading nations in the world. The slave trade was a great economic boon to powerful and wealthy businessmen in England. They held much sway in politics, and Wilberforce knew that it would be political suicide to fight for the abolition of slave trade in England. But as a true kingdom person, he put kingdom virtues over personal gain and dedicated his life to eliminating slave trade from the British marketplace. After long years of concentrated effort, he succeeded. He never became prime minister of England, but his name stands larger today than all the prime ministers of his day. And more than that, he demonstrated for all the world to see that there are virtues that transcend power, fame, wealth, and earthly acclaim. He was an admirable kingdom representative.

7. Humility

The seventh principle of kingdom living that becomes a virtuous expression of our allegiance to the King is *humility*, in place of haughty self-exaltation. Again the king dramatically demonstrates this kingdom virtue for us, since if anyone didn't need to be humble it was Him. Yet the King of glory, the Creator of the universe, humbled Himself to maximize His effectiveness in fulfilling His Father's plan.

The first thing to note about this particular kingdom virtue is that it is a choice, not a state of being. So often we envision true humility as a temperament or a particular persona that we carry around with us. If we are quiet, unassuming, undemanding, frail, and easily victimized and carry all of this with a kind and sweet spirit, then we are truly humble. Interestingly, I sometimes sense that some people who assume this type of humility are quite proud of how humble they have become. It would actually be possible for someone to be rather bold, courageous, clearly articulate, and highly effective who at the same time manifests a true spirit of humility. In fact, isn't that an exact profile of our King?

True humility relates to two basic choices we make. First, a choice to recognize that all we are and all we accomplish is due only to the fact that someone else has made it possible for us to succeed. True humility gives credit to Someone who is above and beyond ourselves, without whose assistance and provision we could do nothing. Second, true humility chooses to humble its will in submission to a higher moral authority. In simple terms, truly humble people obey. Not only in the realm of active choices, but also in their acceptance of the places, positions, and lots in life that our Supreme Authority in His sovereignty assigns for His divine purposes.

I find it interesting that Christ consistently spoke of doing all that He did for the glory of His Father in heaven. In John 9, as He was getting ready to heal the blind beggar, He proclaimed that the man had been born blind that the works of God might be displayed in Him. He might have been tempted to glorify Himself through the miracle, but instead He focused the attention on the power of God the Father through His life. In fact, Christ gave up His own glory to come to this earth where He was misrepresented, marginalized, rejected, impoverished, and criminalized in order that His Father might be glorified through the redemptive rescue of those whom Satan had captured for his own domain. So evident to Christ was this loss of personal glory that He prayed in His high priestly prayer (John 17) that the Father might eventually restore the glory that He had forfeited to come here on earth.

Our King also demonstrated true humility by not only giving His Father the glory and accepting God's assignment for Him in His homeless predicament on this planet, but He also was willing to obey His Father all the way to the cross. Paul underscores this aspect of true humility when he writes that Christ "humbled Himself by becoming obedient to the point of death, even death on a cross" (Phil. 2:8).

What then do we make of our search for exaltation? The domain through which we are passing in a sense allows for exaltation to come when we demand it by haughtily promoting ourselves. In the world of the kingdom, exaltation comes in God's time and in God's way. After Paul states that Christ humbled Himself, in Philippians 2, the assurance is given that God the Father ultimately will exalt His Son. For those of us who are kingdom travelers, Peter admonishes us to "humble yourselves, therefore, under the mighty hand of God, that He may exalt you at the proper time, casting all your anxiety upon Him, because He cares for you" (1 Peter 5:6–7). Interestingly enough, this is written just before the famous verse that claims that our adversary, the devil, goes about seeking to devour us. Then the passage goes on to say that those to whom Peter is writing are suffering great persecution and that they must be careful not to seek to remove themselves from their plight out of a desire for self-enhancement but must humbly continue to be used of God.

True humility, living for God's glory and the gain of His kingdom in a spirit of unquestioned obedience, is a principle that affects our behavior and moves our attitudes and responses toward that which is truly righteous. We live for the glory of a righteous God and follow the directives of a God who cannot tell us to do anything but that which is truly righteous.

As professional golfer Bernard Langer sank the putt on the eighteenth hole to win the coveted Master's title, he walked off the green and was given the green blazer that only a select few are able to wear. A national TV reporter began with the statement, "This must be the greatest day of your life!" It happened to be Easter Sunday, and Bernard Langer replied, "This is the greatest day in my golf career, but I have to say that it doesn't compare with the fact that two thousand years ago on this day my Lord and Savior Jesus Christ rose from the dead to give me life eternal."

A CONCERT OF VIRTUOUS LIVING

All seven of these kingdom virtues mingle in a beautiful concert of character and impact for the King. Rarely do they stand independent and alone. Love will motivate grace, justice, and servanthood. Justice will need truth, grace, humility, and love to guard it from becoming cold, cruel, and misdirected. Self-control will need truth to guide it and humility to protect it from pride and judgmental attitudes. And, while all of these produce the righteous style of the kingdom, they are rooted in an unwavering allegiance to Christ who exemplifies their application in this present world.

These are the virtues by which kingdom travelers are measured. They create the grid through which all our decisions are made. They are the essence of eternity in us expressed through us. They are the key to character and our insulation from the consequences of the earth-side values that constantly seek to erode and deteriorate personal stability, satisfaction, and meaningful relationships.

Note the contrast between the principles of the kingdom and the principles of this present world system by reviewing the chart "The Kingdom Virtues vs. Earth-side Values" on pages 182–83.

THE KINGDOM VIRTUES VS.

Character	Kingdom Virtue
Opposed to falsehood and sin Committed to biblical absolutes Open to conviction Confident in what is true	*Truth*
Uses power and resources to empower others to succeed Generous Merciful Forgiving	*Grace*
Caring toward others Compassionate Shares goods and resources Sacrificing and longsuffering	*Love*

Uses position to enhance
    and advance others
Attentive to others' needs
Seeks to serve others
Views resources as means
    of helping others
	Servanthood

Discerning and disciplined Determined Peaceful, safe	*Self-Control*
Seeks to relieve the oppressed Protects others Promotes equality of mankind	*Justice*
Gives credit where due Accepts assigned place Meek Obedient Grateful	*Humility*

EARTH-SIDE VALUES

Earth-side Value	Consequences
Tolerance	Tolerant of falsehood and sin Pragmatic Closed to conviction Vacillating

Greed	Uses power and resources
	   for personal gain at
	   others' expense
	Ruthless
	Vengeful

Self-Centeredness	Preoccupied with self Compassionless Hoards goods and resources Resists sacrifice and suffering
Significance	Seeks noticeable and affirmed significance Insensitive to others' needs Expects others to serve self Materialistic
Sensualism	Vulnerable to every impulse and addiction Irresolute Victimized by results of sin

Oppression	Victimizes weak for
	   personal gain
	Ruins others to enhance
	   self
	Promotes racial and ethnic
	   strife; economic decline

Haughtiness	Takes credit to self Envious, jealous Arrogant and assertive Insubordinate Grumbling

The sign that we have indeed been delivered from the domain of darkness and deposited into the kingdom of His dear Son is the increasing evidence that we have embraced these virtues that are so clearly expressed by our King. Christlikeness is the result of an inner world managed by the King. The ultimate compliment we can receive in this life is to be noticed as being like the King.

Though these virtues are principles that govern and direct all that we do, Christ our King extends their application to specific *perspectives* and *practices* that characterize a pilgrim whose heart is fixed on paradise. In the Sermon on the Mount He answers the question, "What does my daily routine look like in attitude and action when I live by kingdom virtues?"

CHAPTER FIFTEEN

KINGDOM PERSPECTIVES AND PRACTICES

THE SERMON IN OUR LIVES

Most heated discussions end in the verbal standoff, "Well, let's face it, we just have a different point of view." How is it that one person can see fishing as the most boring pastime in the world and shopping as the most thrilling event of a weekend? It is beyond most men's comprehension. It's a matter of perspective. It affects everything. How we look at life, music, fashion, and friends is determined by our point of view.

Those of us in tune with the world within not only realize that we have changed places and embraced a new set of principles, but that we also have an entirely new perspective on life. A point of view that revolutionizes both our way of thinking and acting. Those of us who are committed to expressing the virtues of the kingdom within must move toward an eager understanding and adoption of the perspectives and resultant practices of the kingdom experience.

I grew up as a pastor's kid, sometimes unaffectionately called a "P.K." I'd like to have a five-dollar bill for every time someone said, "Young man . . ." and I always knew I was in trouble when they started like that . . . "you're the pastor's son. You should set the example for the other children." Quite frankly, though I was happy to accept all the advantages and privileges of being the pastor's son, I had little or no interest in modifying my behavior to be consistent with my identity. Actually, to "be good" was not what I wanted to be. I was full of fun and mischief like every other kid, and conformity was a burden.

If we are not properly focused, as kingdom travelers we will share a lot in common with the plight of the P.K. We revel in the perks of the kingdom—significance, security, freedom from ultimate despair—but often struggle with allegiance and conformity to the perspectives and practices of the kingdom. But, unlike burdened pastoral offspring, when we get a grip on the reality of eternity and the superiority of the kingdom, particularly in contrast to the consequences of life according to this present world, living from a kingdom point of view becomes a privilege, not a problem.

A DECLARATION FROM THE KING

As I have noted, the coming of Christ brought the culture of the kingdom into clear focus, particularly in terms of how it is lived out in this present world. Nowhere is it more clear than in the book of Matthew which, more than the other gospels, features the theme of Christ as King. And nowhere are the details of kingdom perspectives and practices more specific than in Christ's Sermon on the Mount (Matthew 5–7). The Sermon on the Mount was, as some have termed it, the ordination sermon for the disciples, charting for them the distinctive nature of kingdom behavior. From an earth-side point of view this sermon is a radical expression of the kingdom in contrast to the normal patterns of life in this dark domain. One scholar has called the Sermon on the Mount the "Magna Carta of the Kingdom."

Unfortunately, many have felt that the Sermon on the Mount was Christ's prophetic statement about what life will be like in the literal millennial kingdom when He comes to reign on this earth. And while that is certainly true, it ignores the fact that the perspectives and practices portrayed in this sermon are eternal qualities that emanate from the very nature of the King Himself. It would be a gross distortion of the eternal nature of righteousness to say that we can ignore this kingdom point of view and wait to express these perspectives when He reigns as King on the earth. He reigns as King within our hearts *now*. We, as His subjects, live presently under His authority and as such portray a glad submission of all we are and have.

To be specific, the Sermon on the Mount delineates ten life *perspectives* that translate into clear kingdom *practices* in our lives. These ten perspectives form our attitude and action in every area of life and express an accurate reflection of the King who reigns within. The ten categories deal with a radically different perspective on *people;* a new sense of *purpose;* unique perspectives on *personal relationships; personal piety; prosperity; inner peace; personal accountability; prayer; spiritual perception;* and the *authority of Christ's proclamation.* Not unlike the Ten Commandments, these ten perspectives of the kingdom become a means of managing the world within and also measure how far we have come in terms of kingdom behavior. They create, as well, a point of accountability by which we can ultimately give a good report to the King.

THE KING'S POINT OF VIEW

Before we can hope to apply our King's point of view, there are six keys that enable us to both understand the meaning of the sermon and the effective implementation of the perspectives. First, Christ intended that *eternity* be kept in clear view. If there is no world beyond, then little in the sermon makes sense. For instance, you can give away a coat if the possessions that truly count are already reserved for you in heaven. If there is a better, safer, longer life beyond, then the sermon's demands on our lives are reasonable and applicable. Second, since *righteousness* is the centerpiece of Christ's rule, it becomes the highest law in every deliberation of life. If we are to err in any direction, we should lean toward that which advances righteousness rather than that which would give ground to unrighteousness in our lives or the lives of others. According to the sermon, it would be better to be personally taken advantage of than to give cause for another to act unrighteously. Third, throughout this kingdom proclamation Christ views life from the priority of that which is *internal.* In contrast to the religious environment of His day, He moves beyond the outward scenery to the inner landscape. With the King, people are like good fruit. It's not how good they look on the outside; it's the inside that validates the quality. Fourth, it is clear that the sermon values that which is *spiritual* over that which is material and temporal. Given a choice, the kingdom perspective always defers to the former. The soul is of greater priority. Fifth, we must understand and welcome the *tension* that is inherent in Christ's teaching. Christ is imposing the standards of a perfectly pure kingdom culture onto a fallen and treacherous world. If at times the sermon seems to contradict this present world's sense of what is reasonable, it is because this world's point of view is inevitably in conflict with the kingdom culture of Christ. The fault is not with the sermon but with the imperfect world. True wisdom belongs to the King. The sixth and final key in applying the perspectives and practices that are taught in the sermon is that *we should not expect God to treat us in ways that we are unwilling to treat others.* If we are ruthless, unforgiving, and evil with others, then it is presumptuous for us to plead with God to be patient, tolerant, kind, and forgiving with us.

These then are the six grids through which this sermon must be filtered, as we seek to understand and implement its teaching.

PRACTICING WHAT HE PREACHED

This sermon is, in effect, the manual for managing the world within. The chart "Kingdom Perspectives and Practices" on pages 202–3 summarizes the ten perspectives and their resultant practices. These guidelines are the essence of what it means to express eternity through the daily management of our lives. No one will be able to ignore the reality of a righteous, conquering King when our redeemed world within is governed by these practices.

1. Getting People in Perspective

The first and most famous section of the Sermon on the Mount gives us a clear kingdom perspective on *people*. This section, commonly known as the Beatitudes (Matt. 5:1–12), creates a dramatically different picture of who the truly blessed people are in this present world. The world to which Christ came was not much different than the world through which we travel. Blessedness, or happiness, in this present world is defined by wealth, power, comfort, good health, and the capacity to define and realize our own dreams. Those who achieve these goals are marked as the best and the blessed in this present world. Those who never quite make it are the unimportant, weak, and unfortunate. Christ dramatically reorients our point of view. He declares that those who are poor in spirit . . . those who mourn . . . the gentle . . . those who hunger and thirst for righteousness . . . the merciful . . . the pure in heart . . . the peacemakers . . . and those who are persecuted for the sake of righteousness are the truly blessed.

There is an interesting twist to the word Christ uses for "blessed." It is the Greek word that means "happy." And interestingly enough, the Isle of Cyprus, which was an island with a great climate, bountiful flowers and fruits, rich minerals, and abundant natural resources, was known as "the happy Isle." No doubt the Caribbean of their day. The word used here about the blessedness of life is the word that the Greeks used when they spoke of Cyprus. The wealthy had elaborate homes on the island, and the poor and estranged flocked there to provide their services as servants. These underclass people seemed anything but blessed by contrast to the wealthy island residents. That would not only be true in Cyprus but throughout the land of Israel, where blessedness was interpreted by material and physical prosperity, and a lack of such would reflect a lack of blessing.

Christ, however, claims that from a kingdom point of view those who seem to be anything but blessed are in reality the blessed ones. Christ specifically notes why. Earth-side blessedness is but a fleeting ecstasy. Then like fireworks on the Fourth of July it becomes merely a trace of smoke in the sky—in fact a prelude to significant loss on the other side if we are not found in Jesus Christ. But those who suffer loss and disempowerment in this present world have a clearer hope for eternity where blessedness is secured for them. In fact, they more easily can believe in the value of what is to come since there is so little for them here.

The poor in spirit are those whose hearts are fixed on the prosperity that the King provides eternally. Since they have confidence in Christ and Him alone, theirs is the kingdom of heaven. Those who mourn are confident that throughout eternity they will know the comfort of God. That is certainly superior to a griefless life here and an eternity of mourning. The gentle here are those who respond in grace and forgiveness to their offenders. They are those who do not use their power for revenge against their enemies. As such they are vulnerable and suffer measures of loss. Yet they will inherit possessions that cannot be taken from them. As Christ said, "They shall inherit the earth."

In a world where people hunger and thirst to satisfy their lusts with evil, Christ says it is those who passionately pursue righteousness who will ultimately find satisfaction.

The merciful will find mercy with God.

In a world that celebrates the capacity to manipulate life in sinful ways, Christ elevates those who by contrast are pure in their motives, for, as He points out, they shall know intimacy with God.

In contrast to those who use intimidation and disruption to gain selfish ends, Christ said that those who live to make peace are known throughout eternity as sons of God, since God Himself is the ultimate peacemaker.

Those who have defined their lives by the virtues of the kingdom and suffered persecution from a world that hates the principles of paradise will remain unshaken because heaven will be eternally theirs. As Christ concludes this section He reminds us that for those of us who are persecuted for righteousness, "your reward in heaven is great" (Matt. 5:12).

The practices that grow out of this unique eternal perspective on people are many. Let's look at two. First, it radically alters how I look at others. This perspective changes me in terms of who I admire and seek to emulate. In this world it is easy to admire the powerful and to follow in their way. But a kingdom person looks at people differently. The people I admire around me are those who have honor in kingdom terms. They become objects of my respect and affirmation. Those who are truly blessed become an object of my embrace, not embarrassment.

Second, this perspective drives me to value above all else righteousness, mercy, purity, peace, and perseverance.

I am now aware that focusing my passions on righteousness will prepare my heart to know the satisfaction of the righteousness that will characterize and dominate all of eternity. I will develop patterns of righteous living here. And, in fact, I will avoid the regret that comes from unrighteousness, which actually erodes fulfillment.

Knowing that God is determined to show mercy toward those who are merciful encourages me to practice mercy in all my relationships.

Understanding this perspective on life should motivate us to be pure in heart. Which means that as a kingdom person I measure my motives by the righteous standards of the kingdom.

As a kingdom person my view of life will be to pursue peace and promote peace in my relationships, that I might reflect that character of my King, peacemaking Jesus.

And, if I am misunderstood, maligned, or marginalized—physically or mentally persecuted because I am fully committed to the virtues and practices of righteousness and accurately reflect my place in the kingdom—then I will not be shaken. Because I have the confidence that though they may take everything from me here, the kingdom of heaven will be ultimately mine.

These perspectives on life obviously make a dramatic difference in the practice of my life.

2. Purpose in Life

The second perspective that radically alters our practice in life as a kingdom traveler deals with a revised definition of the *purpose* of life. Christ goes on in this sermon (Matt. 5:13–16) to relate that we are to live as salt and light in this world. Salt functions as a flavoring agent. It seems evident that Christ is saying that our practice in this present world needs to deepen and bring richer, truer taste to life. From the context, obviously this is done by living out the principles of the kingdom. In a sense, living out the uniqueness of kingdom virtues and perspectives enhances an otherwise tasteless world.

Salt has a preserving element as well. During Jesus' day, many of the soldiers received part of their pay in salt, a valuable commodity that would preserve their food from spoiling. As salt preserved meat, so kingdom people are to preserve truth by promoting the principles of righteousness. When we manage our world within in a way that expresses the kingdom practices of righteousness, we function as a preservative in this present world. Through a righteous presence in both proclamation and practice, we help to preserve the sanity and safety that only comes when a society lives righteously. The salt of our righteousness preserves an otherwise decaying world through parents who rear godly children; employers who apply biblical ethics toward their employees; voters who support righteous causes; citizens who cry out against violence and injustice.

Kingdom subjects live out this kingdom purpose as lights in the darkness. Our "light" is the impact that our good works (v. 16) have on this dark domain. Good works are not nice, Boy Scout types of things. While good works may at times be nice, and while they may involve helping an elderly person across the street, they are deeper and more significant than that. In Scripture good works are the result of a non-negotiated commitment to righteousness. They are the outcomes of a life fully submitted to the authority of the King. Since Christ the King is unquestionably good and can be nothing but good, when I submit myself to Him then only that which is good emanates from my life. Christ notes that our good works cut like beams of light through the darkness of the world in which we live. Like cities set on a hill we cannot help but be noticed. And as people see us, even though they may not want to listen to us, these good works become so compelling in contrast to the despairing results of their unrighteousness that they will at the least admit that there is something unique about our lives. As the text notes, in many cases they too will come to seek and know the King and glorify Him with us.

Shortly after World War II, Europe began picking up the pieces. Much of the old country had been ravaged by war and was in ruin. Among the rubble, little orphaned children begged for food and sometimes starved in the streets of those war-torn cities.

Early one chilly morning an American soldier in London was returning to his barracks. From his Jeep he spotted a little lad with his nose pressed to the window of a pastry shop. Pastor and author Charles Swindoll tells what happened next:

> Inside, the cook was kneading dough for a fresh batch of doughnuts. The hungry boy stared in silence, watching every move. The soldier pulled his Jeep to the curb, stopped, got out, and walked quietly over to where the little fellow was standing. Through the steamed-up window he could see the mouth-watering morsels as they were being pulled from the oven, piping hot. The boy released a light groan as he watched the cook place them inside the glass-enclosed counter.
>
> The soldier's heart went out to the nameless orphan as he stood beside the boy.
>
> "Son, would you like one of these?"
>
> The boy was startled.
>
> "Oh yeah . . . I would!" he said.
>
> The American stepped inside and bought a dozen, put them in a bag, and walked back to where the boy was standing. He smiled, held out the bag, and said, "Here you are."[1]

According to Swindoll, the GI had turned and begun to walk away when he felt his coat being pulled. He looked around to see the child at his side.

"Mister, are you Jesus?" the little boy asked.

Like that GI, we're never more like Jesus than when we submit to righteous impulses and do what is good and right. That is what light in darkness means. When we are fully devoted to the King, our light and good works ultimately will conquer the darkness.

3. Personal Relationships

The third aspect of a kingdom perspective deals with *personal relationships*—particularly those difficult and challenging relationships (Matt. 5:21–48). Initially, since it must govern all our relational initiatives, righteousness is at the very heart of the kingdom. Anything that elicits actions or responses that are unrighteous is avoided even when that choice creates loss to us and violates what we think are our rights and privileges. Avoiding all appearances of unrighteousness is what is truly right for the kingdom person.

It is important to note as well that this intriguing segment of the sermon is clearly focused on that which is internal. Christ notes that we can be conformed to righteousness in our actions while destructive attitudes remain within us. As such we are guilty. The Jews in Christ's day had so structured their system of religious ethics that measurements for righteousness were merely external. This, needless to say, enabled a person to appear upright on the outside, but remain relationally corrupt on the inside.

This, in fact, is exactly why Jesus accused the religious leaders of being "whitewashed sepulchers." To the Jews in that day, anything having to do with death was defiled. Touching a grave during the feast days, when they were required to be ceremonially pure, would be one disqualifying defilement, for example. So the Pharisees would whitewash the sepulchers around Jerusalem to enable them to stand out so that others could avoid even the slightest unintentional contact with the defiling influence. This background adds tremendous weight to Christ's accusation of the Pharisees' externally clean posture. In reality they were deeply defiled and disqualified because of what was on the inside.

Keeping that in mind, Christ compels us to (1) avoid any relational action that encourages unrighteousness and (2) be sure our attitude on the inside is right in every personal relationship. Christ clearly delineates several scenarios that compel us to kingdom expressions in our personal relationships.

Everyone knows that if you hate your brother to the extent that you kill him, you are guilty of murder. What we rarely admit, however, is that if we hate to that extent, we are guilty as well. Christ goes on to say that if this anger leads us to speak words that kill a person's reputation and murder his sense of worth, then that too makes us liable for judgment (verses 1–22). Kingdom behavior deals with our anger by letting God deal with our enemies. Instead of harboring anger and seeking revenge with vengeful words, we pursue righteousness in our relationships, even with those who have offended us and caused us to feel angry.

The Last Supper by Leonardo da Vinci is one of the great Renaissance masterpieces. During the time da Vinci was painting this masterwork, he reportedly became incensed with a certain man. His temper flared, and he lashed out with bitter words.

Returning to his work, he attempted to brush some delicate lines on the face of Jesus. But he was so distraught that he couldn't regain his composure. Unable to continue, he finally left his tools and went to look for the man and ask his forgiveness. Only after his apology was accepted and he felt right with God could the artist go back and complete the face of Christ.

While we don't know if that story is true, we do know it makes a valid point: Our relationship with other people affects our relationship with God.

Christ goes on to note that people who are truly committed to the kingdom do not worship their King in the midst of offense to others. If we have done something offensive, He calls us to go immediately to the one we have offended and humbly seek to reconcile. When that has happened, we can resume our worship to the King.

If I have so deeply offended another that I am taken to court, and if indeed I am guilty, before going to court I must seek to restore what is rightly his and a righteous relationship with him. As Christ said, I am to make him my friend.

For husbands and wives, Jesus gave specific commands about proper relationships. Not unlike Christ's statement about murder, it was obvious to everyone in Judaism that if you committed adultery you were morally guilty before God. Christ now deepened the accountability by stating that if you permit adulterous thoughts to reside in your heart then you are already guilty of adultery (verse 28). If we are consumed with lust and the only thing that keeps us from committing adultery is the lack of opportunity or the fear of getting caught, we are adulterous (verse 28). A person who fantasizes about immorality, even though he or she never finds an opportunity, is neither righteous nor guiltless.

In regard to moral compromise in relationships, Christ stresses the importance of righteousness when He states that if our eyes or hands cause us to sin, then we would be better off if we blinded ourselves or cut off our hands, so that our souls would be safe. Christ could not have made a stronger statement about the value of righteous living. Kingdom people value righteousness and spiritual well-being more than sight, dexterity, or anything else in this world.

In relating to our spouses, Christ calls us to faithfulness and loyalty. Jewish law permitted the Jews to indiscriminately divorce their wives. This placed women at great jeopardy. To support themselves in that society, most women who were expelled from marriage had two options: remarriage or sexual promiscuity. When a man divorced his wife, he placed her in jeopardy of remarriage, which in God's eyes was adulterous since their divorce was invalid in the first place. In extreme cases, women were driven to the streets as prostitutes. The only permission that Christ granted for putting away a wife was her continual unchaste behavior. Other than that, Christ called righteous men to protect, patiently live with, and love their wives.

Christ also addressed relating in contractual arrangements. The Jews of Christ's day had a custom of sealing agreements by making an oath against heaven, Jerusalem, or even, as strange as it seems, swearing by "their own head." Christ calls us to be true to our word without appealing to authorities beyond ourselves. Kingdom people speak their word and are faithful to it regardless of the implications. To a kingdom person, a promise is a critical thing and carries the integrity of the one who has spoken it.

In relating to those who set themselves against us, Christ speaks about the importance of defusing evil in the midst of unrighteous circumstances. He notes that while our normal response when we are wronged is revenge, a kingdom person would rather be slapped twice than to return evil by slapping the person back. And if someone sues us for our shirt in court, then we should offer him our coat. If someone forces us to go a mile, then we should offer to go an additional mile. While each of these responses seems to be an unreasonable reaction, the alternative would be grist for deepening hostilities. The kingdom person values peace more than fighting back. He values a relationship more than a shirt. And he is willing to go out of his way to benefit another person. This is revolutionary kingdom behavior.

Soon after the doors opened to the former Soviet Union, the educational leaders in Russia invited U.S. Christian organizations to come and show the film *Jesus* to teachers and train them in values and ethics curriculums based on the Word of

God. A massive group of Christian organizations pooled their resources under the name of "CoMission" in order to accept this invitation. Attendant were opportunities to evangelize teachers, place them in Bible studies, and plant churches.

For two and a half years, more than a thousand believers from the States gave one year of their lives to participate in this project until the Russian Orthodox Church began to pressure the government to keep these "evangelists"—who had come, in their words, "under the guise of education"—out of the schools.

In gestures of goodwill, CoMission had supplied the educational ministry with duplicating machines since upgraded equipment was so scarce during that time. When the edict came from the Ministry of Education that the schools would no longer be open to the work of CoMission, the very machines CoMission had donated were used to duplicate that edict. Halfway through the process they ran out of paper. Since the CoMission had often supplied them with not only the equipment but with reams of paper as well, they asked if they could get more paper.

The earthbound response for the people in charge of that aspect of CoMission's ministry would have been to laugh in their faces, since the Ministry of Education had so ungraciously pulled up the welcome mat. But like a good kingdom people, these CoMission kingdom travelers in Moscow asked how much paper they wanted, and then supplied sufficient paper to finish the project.

It won the hearts of those Russians who by no choice of their own were serving notice to the schools of their land. Had CoMission denied them the paper, they would have been just like everyone else in this present world. Going the extra mile defused the tension in a hostile environment and kept Russian hearts open to the much more significant issue of the gospel of Jesus Christ.

Perhaps the most challenging of contradictions of earth-side relational responses comes next. Christ states that while the common consensus is "you shall love your neighbor and hate your enemy" (which was street talk in their day for "I don't get mad, I just get even"), we are instead to love our enemies and pray for those who persecute us, because in that way we become like our Father who is in heaven.

These perspectives on kingdom relational behavior come into clear view when we recall that the centerpiece of the kingdom is *righteousness* in conflict with a fallen environment—that the kingdom is measured by what's going on *inside* us, and what is *spiritually* right is of greater value than what is personally or physically right.

4. Personal Piety

After speaking about kingdom ways to relate to our fellowman, Christ then went on to lay out how we are to relate to our Father in heaven. This is the fourth kingdom perspective, *personal piety* (6:1–13). This section stands in contrast to the public religious abuse being practiced in that day. This abuse related to the fact that people carried out religious practices for their own gain.

The three areas to which Christ particularly speaks are giving, praying, and fasting. It is interesting that Christ's label for people who give, pray, and fast in order to be noticed and publicly affirmed is *hypocrite.* A hypocrite is someone whose life contradicts the very essence of what he says he believes. Religious practice by nature has its focus outside of and beyond ourselves. The activities in the arena of our faith by their nature are practiced on behalf of God. When we say we are serving God yet our intent is to serve ourselves, we qualify as hypocrites. Doing God's work for our advantage robs God of the glory due to Him. The result of serving ourselves while appearing to serve heaven is that we lose our eternal reward, since we have rewarded ourselves here on earth.

Giving is to be done in secret with no thought of personal gain.

Prayer is to be done in secret, trusting that our Father will hear us and help us in secret. Christ then instructs His disciples in what we know as the Lord's Prayer, which focuses first beyond ourselves to the Father's glory, and then to our fundamental needs of bread, forgiveness, and safety from the treachery of the evil one. It is important here to note the closing focus of this prayer affirms that the kingdom is God's and the power and glory are His as well.

And just in case we don't want to pray "... as we forgive those who trespass against us ..." Christ reminds us that if we are unwilling to forgive others who have offended us, how do we expect to ask Him to forgive us?

When we fast we are not to do so that others will notice how spiritual we are by our gaunt and frail appearance. Because fasting is a personal thing between my Father and myself, we are to fast in secret and disguise the fact that we are fasting. It is something that only God needs to know. Subjects of the kingdom value the intimate relationship they have with their King and practice piety for His glory and not their own.

5. Prosperity

Few things jeopardize Christians more than the promise of *prosperity*. Kingdom living gives us a new perspective on prosperity (6:19–24). It is impossible for us as kingdom adherents to dedicate ourselves to money and at the same time to dedicate ourselves to God. Christ points out that the folly of dedicating ourselves to money is that earth-side treasure is susceptible to damage and demise. Radical changes in economy, personal crises, forays into speculative investments—all can create sudden loss. If we are not careful we might build our security on the accumulation of these slippery assets. On the other hand, Christ teaches that kingdom people use their prosperity to stack up treasures on the other side where the gain is permanent and of greater value.

On this issue Christ notes that if our view of prosperity is dictated by the perspectives of this fallen world, then the darkness within is deep. And it is deep indeed. Its ramifications touch every area of our lives. The pursuit of money for money's sake damages family relationships and creates pride when we succeed and despair when we fail.

6. Peace

Granted, shifting our focus on prosperity from money to eternal treasures may create anxiety in terms of being able to provide for our needs. At this point, Christ turns kingdom hearts toward His *peace*. He reminds us that our Father in heaven obviously cares that our needs are met. Christ points to the birds of the air and the flowers of the field that are wonderfully cared for by God, and then He calls us to seek first the things of eternity, assuring us that the Father knows our needs. He also encourages us to live each day focusing on the advance of the kingdom without worrying about the needs of tomorrow. Kingdom people know that today is ours to live for the kingdom, and tomorrow belongs to the King who will provide and care for us when and if tomorrow comes.

The great preacher Charles H. Spurgeon once learned about such peace while trying to raise money for poor children in London. He came home to Bristol hoping to collect 300 pounds to support his work with London's homeless children. At the end of the week of meetings, many lives had been changed and his financial goal had been reached. That night as he bowed in prayer, Spurgeon seemed to hear a voice saying, "Give that money to George Mueller" (the founder of a great orphanage in England). "Oh, no, Lord," answered the preacher, "I need it for my own dear orphans."

Yet Spurgeon couldn't shake the idea that God wanted him to part with it. Only when he said, "Yes, Lord, I will," could he find rest.

With great peace, he made his way the next morning to Mueller's orphanage and found that great man of prayer on his knees. The famous minister placed his hand on Mueller's shoulder and said, "George, God has told me to give you these 300 pounds I've collected."

"Oh, my dear brother," said Mueller, "I've just been asking Him for exactly that amount."

The two servants of the Lord then wept and rejoiced together. When Spurgeon returned to London, he found a letter on his desk containing 300 guineas. "There," he cried with joy, "the Lord has returned my 300 pounds with 300 shillings interest!"

Spurgeon learned what another generous believer once said, "I shovel out, and God shovels in, and He has a bigger shovel than I do."

7. Taking It Personally

The next perspective on kingdom living focuses on *personal accountability*. For those of us who focus on the faults of others (and no doubt by comparison feel good about ourselves), Christ calls us to manage our own responsibilities. Christ again calls it a form of hypocrisy when we stand in judgment of others when we ourselves need to be judged. He underscores that we have the right to deal with others' faults only when we have dealt with our own, and, in fact, that we will be judged by the standard we set for others. As I have noted, throughout the sermon there is a sense of reciprocity—we will be treated in the same way that we treat others. We will receive mercy to the same degree that we are merciful. We will be rewarded from heaven when we reward heaven with our personal affections. We will be forgiven as we forgive. And here, we will be judged by the same standard that we judge others.

After warning us to make sure that we have judged ourselves before we judge others, Christ cautions us to be careful even with whom we seek to purify. He states that some are incorrigible and beyond remediation of their faults. Like dogs or swine, they devour the words we offer them about what is holy and right. If someone is evil to the core, then we should keep that which is holy and precious to ourselves and not seek to reprove him with words of righteousness.

8. Dependence

Kingdom people have a radically different perspective about who's in charge. It's not them. In a world where independence is considered strength, as followers of the King we do not depend on our own plans, but on God's (7:7–11). Our plans can fail, but God's plans never fail.

Because God is in charge, the kingdom follower consults God often. Prayer is the primary expression of *dependence* on God. We come to Him regularly, as Jesus did, to find both counsel and comfort. When we make prayer a priority in our daily lives, we show that we trust God will answer and that His answers will benefit our well-being.

Given the confidence that our Father in heaven is even more gracious than our earthly fathers, Christ encourages us to pray with clear requests.

KINGDOM PERSPECTIVES AND PRACTICES
(from Matthew 5–7)

Earth-side Perspectives	Kingdom Perspectives	Kingdom Practices: Attitudes and Actions
Blessedness is in position, power, wealth, comfort, safety, and acceptance in this domain	1. Blessedness is in the assurance of ultimate comfort, reward, and intimacy in eternity (5:1–12)	• Be aware that happiness is a long-range reality • Honor and affirm those who are truly blessed • Accept present lot in life in terms of its eternal reward
Purpose in life is to enhance and advance self in terms of personal peace and prosperity	2. Purpose in life is to advance the cause of our king by functioning as flavor preservatives and light in a flat, decaying, and dark environment (5:13–20)	• Affirm righteousness • Actively search for occasions to create hunger and thirst for God • Actively attempt to stop decay
Relationships are used for personal benefit	3. Relationships are to remain pure, blameless, fair to the weak, and forgiving to enemies (5:21–48)	• Seek the unquestion-ably right way to feel and act in every situation • Make my rights or safety secondary to doing what is right
Good works are paraded for personal glory	4. Personal piety means the focus is on private devotion to God (6:1–18)	• Spend much time in the quiet and secret develop-ment of my relationship with God • Meditate on ways to show His glory through my life
Prosperity comes by what I accumulate and gain	5. True prosperity comes by contributing to eternity and the advance of Christ's kingdom (6:19–24)	• Seek to advance eternity with all I possess • Give my time and energy to activities that in some way impact eternity

KINGDOM PERSPECTIVES AND PRACTICES
(from Matthew 5–7)

Earth-side Perspectives	Kingdom Perspectives	Kingdom Practices: Attitudes and Actions
Life is lived on the edge of anxiety, fearing that all could be gone instantly	6. Life is lived in peace, knowing that only eternal commodities are secure and worth pursuing (6:25–34)	• Trust God to care for me in His way and His time • Cast all my cares on Him
Personal actions are excused by comparing, blaming, and judging others	7. I am accountable for personal actions before I can reprove others (7:1–6)	• Focus on personal faults and take steps to remediate them • Use discretion with whom to share reproving words of righteousness
Self-sufficient behavior questions the goodness or concern of God	8. God-dependent behavior, as expressed through prayer, relies on the goodness of our Father (7:7–12)	• Let prayer rule my life • Trust God's loving responses to meet my basic needs, regardless of the outcomes
Life is structured to be as natural, comfortable, and as acceptable to the majority as possible	9. Life requires a willingness to endure difficulties and being often in the minority (7:13–23)	• Choose to accept kingdom alternatives that are out of step with the majority • Live by the narrow, right way even though it brings discomfort
Personal drives and desires are the authority in our lives	10. The King's Word, the Bible, is the authority in our lives (7:24–29)	• Display unquestioned loyalty to the King • Obey gladly the decrees of the King

9. Minority Living

Christ brings His kingdom teaching toward a conclusion by reminding us that our *spiritual perception* must accurately reflect the authentic kingdom way and those who represent it. The kingdom way is narrow, and the gate to the kingdom is small. In reality, the narrow way leads to life, and few find it because they prefer the broad way. He warns us of the fact that many false prophets will seek to mislead us and deter us from the narrow way. But their lack of spiritual wisdom is revealed by the outcome of their lives. In fact, they should be measured by the kingdom principles of this sermon. He goes on to warn us that not everyone who claims that Christ is Lord is truly a part of the kingdom.

10. Permanence of the Proclamation

Last, King Jesus calls us to build our lives on the *permanence* of His proclamation. The authority of God's Word is absolute. We are called to consistently obey what He has taught us. He likens those who establish their lives on the perspectives of this sermon to a man who builds his house on a firm foundation. But those who hear Christ's words and refuse to obey are like a man who, having built his life on shifting sand, is in jeopardy when God's final judgment comes.

These then are the perspectives and practices of kingdom life. They are grounded in the reality of eternity, the priority of righteousness, the primacy of the internal, the distinct tension of kingdom life in a different fallen world, the supremacy of the spiritual over the material, and the reality of the fact that we can only expect God to treat us as we treat others.

Christ's sermon is the manual for managing the kingdom world within. It is the quintessential expression of what it means to live in light of the world to come under the authority of the King. It is eternity expressed in our window of history.

Use the "Kingdom Perspectives and Practices" chart as a mirror. See your life as it is now through the flow of this chart. How well do you perceive and practice life from the King's point of view? Then, to apply your specific life situations to the listed perspectives, answer the following four questions:

1. How do you score in kingdom attitudes and actions? (Consider your specific attitudes and actions at home and work.)
2. Is your life characterized more by the earth-side perspectives?
3. Which areas of your life need to be transitioned from the domain of darkness to reflect the kingdom of His dear Son?
4. What can you do to begin the transition?

Those who are driven and defined by the principles of the kingdom, who manage their lives in accordance with kingdom perspectives and practices, will penetrate the darkness with the light of eternity. The kingdom has a culture. Eternity has a style. And those of us who have been transferred from the domain of darkness into the kingdom of His dear Son have the privilege and the responsibility to give our dying world a sneak preview of the really big show to come. Our challenge is to express the triumph of the kingdom world within amid the trouble in this present fallen world.

PART FOUR
THIS PRESENT WORLD

Martin Luther had it right when he wrote, "... this world, with devils filled, should threaten to undo us." It is a truth we are prone to forget, and that in itself is our undoing. Beelzebub's plan for this planet is that its Creator be defamed and defaced by the destruction that he can bring to its environment and its pinnacle commodity: the human race. Hence all the tension and trouble.

Yet for kingdom travelers this present world becomes a platform where we are privileged to display the essence of eternal triumph in the midst of its challenges and pain.

As Luther concluded, "We will not fear, for God hath willed His truth to triumph through us."

It is our privilege as citizens of eternity to live triumphantly here in the light of there on behalf of the King who reigns within.

CHAPTER SIXTEEN

TENSION

WHAT TO EXPECT IN
THIS PRESENT WORLD

Our tough neighborhoods in Chicago are full of treachery, fear, and despair. Their legacies are shame and guilt. Their dead-end streets and alleys are places where residents have been lured to strike deals and sell their souls for personal gain, only to find that regret and loss are the ultimate payoff.

Spiritually speaking, the world in its present configuration is a nasty neighborhood—regardless of where we live. Soberingly, there is no safe place. Our homes are not safe. Our churches aren't safe. Friendships are not safe. And when I am alone I am not safe. If we could flee to some secluded place, the neighborhood would go with us, for wherever we go this present world goes along. In fact, it's not only around us; it resides within us as well. Until our redemptive passport grants us safe passage to the other side, we will face the *tension* and *trouble* that are inevitably found in this present world. To think of this world as a friend to the kingdom traveler would be the worst deceit of all. In fact, living in light of the world to come in glad allegiance to the King of the world within would be a cakewalk if we didn't have to do it while living in the world around us.

You don't have to tell Scott and Janet Willis that this world is a tough neighborhood in which to live. Their tension and trouble came in maximum doses. Nor do you have to convince the victims of rape, incest, or abuse. The person who has just lost a career or health or who has seen wealth evaporate will readily admit that life here is far less than he or she expected.

I EXPECTED MORE

By far the most important thing for travelers to get into focus is a correct set of *expectations* regarding life in this present world. Failed expectations are the stuff that disillusionment and disappointment are made of. Correct expectations keep us realistic.

Those of us who have children know that raising their expectations and then not delivering can create some traumatic moments at home. I'll never forget the time when our children asked me if I'd take them to the circus when it came to town. Not wanting to be too brutal I said maybe, and promptly forgot about the discussion. Any parent should know that any answer short of a firm "No!" means "Yes." I came home the next Tuesday, and they met me at the door reminding me that this was the night I'd promised to take them to the circus.

I paused. I took a moment to recall their request, and then I blurted out a nonchalant "Oh, I forgot. We're not going to go." They looked at each other, shrugged their shoulders, and went skipping off happily to find something to do.

In my dreams!

They were devastated.

I'm convinced we can trace much of our disappointment in this present world to unrealistic expectations. We grow up expecting a measure of comfort, pleasure, peace, and prosperity. In fact, Francis Schaeffer notes that the desire for personal peace and prosperity is the driving force and fundamental expectation of most Americans. Our problem is not that we want personal peace and prosperity . . . we were built for them. Our problem is that we expect to find them in this present world. And while we may get fleeting glimpses of these commodities, they are less than certain and always less than what we had expected.

Realistic expectations are essential for a successful pilgrimage toward eternity. As I have noted, final, secure, personal peace and prosperity is what the world to come is all about. We can expect it with certainty. What then can we realistically expect here? Scripture speaks of two realities: *tension* and *trouble*. And while God will provide windows of grace where we experience tranquillity, pleasure, and prosperity, a realistic view of life on this planet must understand and expect that life is prone toward encounters with commodities that contradict our hopes and our dreams.

In order to keep our expectations realistic, it is essential to realize why tension and trouble characterize our experience here. The answer relates to the nature of this present world.

WHAT IN THE WORLD IS GOING ON?

Scripture speaks of three distinct definitions of this world. One is the physical world (John 21:25). Scripture also refers to the masses of humanity as the world (John 3:16). Yet it is not the physical planet nor its people that are the *primary* source of tension. The masses of people are only players in a bigger scheme that has its origins in the earliest history of mankind and in the deep recesses of eternity past; here a scheme was born whose power and purposes transcend both this planet and its people. It is this sense of the world that gives us a jolt.

This world is the realm of the King's archenemy, the enemy of our souls—Satan. He uses our planet and its people to wage war against the name and glory of our God who is the unquestioned ruler of the universe. This planet is the platform in the universe where Beelzebub seeks to discredit God. And since we are the pinnacle of God's creation and the capstone of His glory, we make perfect targets and tools in the adversary's effort to defame the divine. We are objects to be used, abused, discarded, and destroyed in the bigger scheme of Satan's purposes. Hence the tension and trouble, and the need for us to learn how to live in the face of carrying the kingdom banner of triumph.

The environment in which we live is manipulated by Satan's purposes, which are energized and executed by the legions of hell. That Satan rules over this realm is clear when Christ calls him the "ruler of this world" (John 12:31). His reign extends to all who are born into this world, since we are all born in sin . . . hopelessly, helplessly separated from God, under the dominion of the "prince of the power of the air" (Eph. 2:1–7). According to Rom. 8:19–22, the whole of creation "groans" under the weight of sin, waiting for redemption when we will be transitioned into the new heavens and the new earth. From metals that rust to storms that destroy, crops that fail, and health that fades—all of creation struggles under the curse of its treacherous ruler.

A FALSE AND FATAL PLACE

Just as the kingdom of Christ has a culture that is governed and defined by the character of the King, so this world has a culture that reflects its dominant influence, Satan. Just as righteousness and conquest characterize the kingdom within, two fundamental ethics characterize his world: *lies* and *violence.* These foundational principles surface in Christ's conversation with the Pharisees. He reveals that their lives are cut from the fabric of this world system since they reflect both of these qualities, for lies and violence are of the prince of this world:

> "But as it is, you are seeking to kill Me, a man who has told you the truth, which I heard from God; this Abraham did not do. You are doing the deeds of your father."
>
> They said to Him, "We were not born of fornication; we have one Father, even God."
>
> Jesus said to them, "If God were your Father, you would love Me; for I proceeded forth and have come from God, for I have not even come on My own initiative, but He sent Me. Why do you not understand what I am saying? It is because you cannot hear My word. You are of your father the devil, and you want to do the desires of your father. He was a murderer from the beginning, and does not stand in the truth, because there is no truth in him. Whenever he speaks a lie, he speaks from his own nature; for he is a liar, and the father of lies." (John 8:40–44)

Note how Christ consistently distances Himself from Satan's world, saying that He is of His Father's world. In fact, in John 17 He reiterates that He is not of this world, nor are His disciples of this world though they live in the midst of it. Christ's world is characterized by truth and life; Satan's, by deceit and death.

Let me explain.

The entire world system is manipulated by lies that ensnare us in Satan's sinister scheme. Lies such as those that lead us to believe that success is measured by credentials rather than character. That happiness comes from liberating ourselves to do whatever seems to bring personal pleasure rather than living a righteous life to please Him. That power is best used to empower our own gain and satisfy our greed. That worth is determined by personal prestige, position, or the roles we play. That money and things are worth more than purity and people. That peace can be found by being in the right places with the right people. That sex is for self. That self is supreme.

Given these lies, it is clear that this world is not only dangerous, but it also isn't in touch with reality. Reality is inseparably linked to what is true. This present world is a fantasy land of false values designed to result in our demise.

Even a casual glance at this world, managed by its prince of darkness, demonstrates the pervasiveness of destruction and death. Crime, random violence, and personal destructive behavior continue to rise. While shopping for Christmas gifts, I noticed a grotesque figure in the toy section. Proudly displayed over its form were the words "Skeletar, Lord of Destruction." Satan is just that. Since the beginning of time, his goals have been destruction and death. No one has ever been or will ever be a better person because of his schemes. Sin debilitates our emotional, spiritual, and physical fiber. We can wrap our inner decay in the grand glitter and style of this world, but the demise of this world's system is inevitable and sure.

And that's just the way Satan likes it. Particularly since a world full of deceit and destruction seems to discredit the Creator who has sovereign control. When was the last time you heard someone blame Satan for the destructive demise of life on this planet? Those who don't know better say, "If there is a God and He is good, then why is there so much misery and pain?" The truth is, God is good and offers life and truth to all who will come to Him. Those who choose to embrace this present world choose Satan's design for their lives. He is to blame.

And God in His wise and perfect time will do something about it, as He judges the prince and all who followed Him and then opens the gates of His eternal world to all the travelers who chose His narrow way. Then all injustice will be rectified and all wrongs made right.

When Scripture speaks of the world under the management of Satan, characterized by lies (non-truth) and violence, it refers to it as the *cosmos*. The *cosmos* is our environment, the land of our pilgrimage; manipulated by our adversary Satan who controls the attitudes and actions of its residents with falsehood, and erodes them slowly but surely with the emptiness of false hopes and the despair of sin.

THE MIDWAY

Circuses were in their heyday when I was a boy. One of the biggest annual events in town was the circus. My dad would take us early in the morning to watch the circus trains unload the tigers, lions, elephants, monkeys, and all the paraphernalia that made the circus so intriguing.

Once the circus was set up, great attractions were lined up along the "midway." The midway was the walk leading to the big tent. Vendors hawked their wares, happy music played, the smell of hot dogs and cotton candy mingled in the air, and multicolored balloons bounced in the wind. With bursts of laughter and screams, customers spun inside a few amusement rides. The midway was almost more than a boy could take.

As my father walked me down the circus midway, the most intriguing sights of all were the "side shows." Large posters advertised all kinds of unique formations of mankind and daring feats of bravery—a man with three eyes, a bearded woman, a six-hundred-pound person, sword swallowers and fire eaters, a man with no arms and no legs.

The barker in front of the side shows added to the intrigue with vivid descriptions of all that waited behind these compelling posters: "For two bits you can see the most amazing wonders of the world. See what no one has ever seen before!" I would pull on my dad's hand and beg him to take me behind the posters so I could see for myself what no one had ever seen before. And my dad would consistently say, "Joe, it's a waste of money. It's not all it's cracked up to be." So I grew up with a longing to see what was behind those posters, to experience what my dad considered wasteful and not worthwhile.

Needless to say, when I was finally on my own I went to a circus—a different kind that was held in a large downtown arena. But sure enough, as I approached the door to the arena, there were the same side shows. By now it cost a dollar to get in, but I gladly paid my buck to see "what no one had ever laid eyes on before."

To my dismay, my father was right; I wasted my money. It wasn't what it was cracked up to be, and I found myself feeling betrayed, having wasted my resources. There were a lot of other things on the midway that were not disappointing—the cotton candy, the two minutes on the Whirleybird, the balloon that stayed on the bedroom ceiling for three days after the circus was over. But other elements were wasteful and disappointing.

The *cosmos* is a lot like the midway. There is much of it that is exciting. But as our Father walks us through the experience, He warns us of what will disappoint us, waste our resources, and in fact distort and destroy us. It's the side shows that seduce us and endanger our experience here.

The world is smooth, slick, and seductive. It consistently puts us in tension with all that it offers. Covetousness creeps into our souls. Its sensual offerings seduce us with promises of instant gratification of our unsatisfied longings. Its possessions, power, and positions promise us significance. It sells us on the proposition that self-enhancement is the chief, most fulfilling pursuit of all. Honest travelers admit that they continually struggle to disentangle themselves from the snares of the midway and must focus and refocus their hearts on the voice of their Father, who guides them through the maze.

The tension forces us to make up our minds about whom we will believe—the barker of the midway? To make up our hearts as to whom we will love—the Father or the faker?

THE TENSION DEFINED

The clearest instruction in Scripture regarding the tension that is explicit in this world is found in 1 John 2:15–17:

> Do not love the world, nor the things in the world. If anyone loves the world, the love of the Father is not in him. For all that is in the world, the lust of the flesh and the lust of the eyes and the boastful pride of life, is not from the Father, but is from the world. And the world is passing away, and also its lusts; but the one who does the will of God abides forever.

The tension directly relates to where we place our love and loyalty.

Loving the *world* means to embrace it, to yield to it, to make it our primary point of allegiance. On my way home from the office I used to regularly pass a florist shop that had a large marquee on its roof advertising special flower deals. I'll never forget passing by one evening and noticing that it said: "Take roses to your main squeeze." I chuckled at the thought of Martie as my "main squeeze."

The real issue on our pilgrimage is who will be our main squeeze. And given what we know about the adversary, loving the Father should be our eager response. Yet many of us are still in love with the world, living for and sacrificing for all it supposedly offers. We seem so ready to yield our careers, our cash, our children, our chastity to the sizzle of the midway. Clearly, love for the Father is not in us when the world has its grip on our heads and our hearts. We can say it, sing it, or even chant about our love for God, but if our choices consistently point to the cosmos rather than the kingdom, then it's clear that we have taken up residence here, having lost our first love (Rev. 2:4–5).

Loving the world means embracing the lies and destructive patterns of this world. Ask the average Christian what success means and you will hear answers about peace, prosperity, position, and power. To most of us success means cars and houses and vacations and credentials. Yet that's the lie proclaimed by the world system. Living for personal gain is an earth-side value that's in direct conflict with eternity's tenets of truth. Shaping life by what's best for *me* is an erroneous perspective of Satan's domain. All of us who have embraced the lies of this world are guilty of loving this world rather than our Father.

We often embrace the violent character of the world. Thus we often are ready to adopt as our own the principles that characterize this system. Gossip and slander are violent actions toward the reputations of others. Anger and revenge destroy relationships as well as rob a sense of worth and dignity from the objects of our anger. Abusive language, physical and sexual abuse are all part of the destructive violence of the *cosmos.* And we can use our power to take advantage of others in an expression of violent impulses.

And what about the way we entertain ourselves with meaningless, random acts of violence on television, videos, and in the movies? Murder, rape, and bloodshed (along with explicit sex most often out of the context of righteousness) have become the draw for big numbers at the box office.

The lies of this world are an insult in the face of a God who is true, and violence is an offense to the created order which God built for His glory and the benefit of mankind. Loving the world by giving allegiance to its lies and destructive influences makes it impossible for us to love God who is true and constructive. It is a contradiction of the eternity in our hearts and our claim to citizenship in the kingdom.

THE TENSION WITH THINGS

John not only calls us away from a love for the world in general, but in particular from the love of the *things* of this world. Things! That's really the point of the struggle. Things we have that we've grown to love more than our Father. Things we wish we had. Things for which we are willing to violate the virtues and practices of the kingdom. Things in the form of clothes, cars, and castles. Things like credentials. Things like men. Things like women. Things like children. Things that cash can buy. Things that give credibility to our power and success.

Almost fifty years ago a young man attending Bible college in Ottawa, Canada, faced the lure of things: cash, fame, and success. His rich baritone voice held audiences spellbound. After an audition at a radio station, the station manager offered the young man a contract. But the manager told him he would be expected to sing Hit Parade songs.

On a Saturday night George Beverly Shea prayerfully considered what he should do. He felt he could commit himself to radio wholeheartedly and Christ halfheartedly or dedicate himself to Christ and sacrifice this once-in-a-lifetime opportunity.

The next morning he sat down at his piano and composed the music and words to a song that he later made famous. He wrote, "I'd rather have Jesus than silver and gold. . . . I'd rather have Jesus than worldwide fame." Those words reflected Shea's choice: Jesus over things.

For George Beverly Shea, following Christ meant saying no to a radio show that might have brought him fame and fortune. Instead, he was willing to sing for Christ in obscurity. Of course, God had a different plan for Shea. Ultimately he would sing to millions around the world as part of the Billy Graham evangelistic team. And his gifts would be used to affect an entire generation for Christ.

Many Christians, though, become so allured by the things of this world that they are willing to love them more than the Father. And it's not that things are intrinsically evil. They aren't. It's when the love for things supplants our love for the Father that we are led to disloyalty and disobedience in order to acquire and enjoy them.

Case in point: the apple in the Garden of Eden.

How do we know if we love things rather than God? We love them more when we are willing to cross the line of loyalty to Him to gain them or indulge in their pleasures. We love them more than Him when we use things for our glory instead of His, for our pleasure at the expense of His, or when they control us instead of Him controlling us.

In the beginning our earth operated in a pleasurable pattern, reflecting Adam and Eve's love for the Father and His worth above the things He had given. All that God created was good. Within the garden was the Tree of Knowledge of Good and Evil of which God asked Adam and Eve not to eat. Their obedience would be an expression that they loved their God more than the things He had created. As long as they lived in love and loyalty toward Him in the midst of all He had created, they experienced the fullness of His pleasure, peace, and prosperity in their environment.

God's intended scheme for a heaven-on-earth experience in Eden had a specific plan. It began with God as Creator relating in unhindered intimacy with His created ones. In turn, they gladly submitted to Him and His plan that they would manage all He had created to bring Him glory. It looked like this:

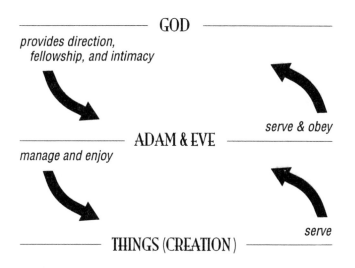

But all of that changed when Satan intruded on what was good and pleasurable. It cannot go without notice that Satan used the *things* of creation to lure the original pair and to place them in subservience to him. It was the created thing, the tree, that lured them. When they loved it more than God, all hell broke loose. Literally. After the temptation and the Fall, the sequence of life on this planet had an entirely new look:

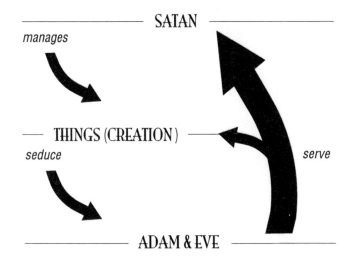

Satan used the things of this world to seduce God's lovers, and when the scheme was executed, the pinnacle of creation lived in both servitude to the things of this world and to the new ruler of the world. The end result was the exclusion of God from the equation. Interestingly, this paradigm shift brought shame and guilt instead of pleasure and prosperity and discredited the worth and glory of God.

The created ones loved the creation more than the Creator, and all have never been the same.

A CHANGE OF MANAGEMENT

At this point we could accurately hang a new sign over our planet, "Under New Management." The world created to the credit and glory of the Almighty God would now be run by the legions of fallen angels under the direction of their leader who, having captured the overseers of the planet, claimed his title as the prince of this world. Management books tell us that organizations reflect their leadership. Leaders who are people/service-oriented create a corporate culture that is consistent with the focus of their lives. Leaders who are profit/product-oriented may, if they aren't careful, create an environment that places product and profit above the worth of its employees and customers. This world is a direct reflection of the personality, purposes, and preferences of its management.

Martie and I have a few favorite spots to go when we want to get away. Since we visit them periodically, we get to know the personnel and look forward to the services they graciously offer. More than once we've returned only to find that the place we loved was under new management. Different people were there with a different quality of service, and, more often than not, we were disappointed.

When we see this present world clearly, we will be disappointed with both its management and services. It's not easy, however, to see clearly. At first glance its attractions are compelling. Satan has hidden his wasteland under the sizzle and seductions of the lights and laughter of this lost and dying world. The sizzle that contradicted the King and the kingdom is what allured Adam and Eve, and they offended the God who was their joy and satisfaction. They loved the creation more than the Creator. Think of the offense of giving so much and then being rejected for so much less. They thought that in having it all they didn't have enough. They loved the gift more than the Giver. They had an affair with a tree and left God standing on the outside of their affections.

Yet God, instead of destroying it all, loved His creation enough to begin the process of restoring it to its original management again. And those of us who are pilgrim travelers now seek to cooperate with that divine agenda by living in loving loyalty to God and managing the things in the creation around us to His glory and gain.

A friend of mine who often travels told me of the time when he checked into a hotel and noticed a rather nice looking woman across the lobby. She was just standing there looking at him. He didn't think much of it and went to his room. As he was unpacking there was a knock at the door. He went to the door and to his surprise this same lady was standing there. She said, "How about if we have a little fun tonight?" What would he do? He was alone. No one would know. This was obviously a moment when the adversary was using God's created handiwork to bring this kingdom traveler across the line of love and loyalty to His God, luring him to serve Satan by submitting himself to the things of this world. Being a man of the kingdom he said, "No, thank you," shut the door, and walked back into his room. He had followed God's original pattern of living in this world by loving the God of creation more than the things that God had created. As such he maintained dominion over what was created that he might please and glorify the Creator.

THE SEDUCTION OF SIZZLELAND

Yet until we are eternally home, the fleeting *things* of creation will be used by our adversary to seduce us into his scheme. He will seek to lure us into this Sizzleland where the love of things that glitter is more important than our love for God. What is important for us to remember is that the Garden of Eden demonstrates that Satan seeks to use the things of this world to place us in servitude to Him.

Crossing the line of love and loyalty for our Creator in order to consume the things of this world for ourselves creates bondage in our lives. The things we think bring us joy soon become our master. Bondage to food, sex, pornography, money, cars, drugs, alcohol, and a host of other addictive forces fuel Satan's ability to destroy our lives. I can't imagine anything worse than to take what seems to be satisfying, to enjoy it, and then to hear a trapdoor slam shut behind me, realizing that what I found enjoyment in has now become the slave master of my life.

That's why John commands us not to yield to the *world*—Satan's system of thinking and living that is characterized by lies and violence. "Neither the things that are in the world"—disloyally giving ourselves to earth-side things which demonstrates that our love for the Father is no longer the ruling reality in our lives.

Not only do we face tension in terms of the things around us, but the tension is felt deeply within us as well.

John warns us that "all that is in the world, the lust of the flesh and the lust of the eyes and the boastful pride of life" are part and parcel of the destructive system of this present world order (1 John 2:16). Interestingly, all of these are felt tensions within us. Which means that this present world is not only around us but in a sense dwells within us as well. This is why fleeing to a mountain or a desert island will never make us feel safe.

THE TENSION WITHIN

The fall in Eden not only changed the environment, but it changed our original parents. Sin resided within them, and the lusts of sin drove them—and now drives us—from the inside out. If God hadn't interrupted the process, mankind would have quickly self-destructed. That potential was put within us when Satan made us sinners after his image. Thankfully for us, God has interrupted our destructive form of living with His gracious and marvelous redemption.

But redemption has not yet canceled all the consequences of the Fall. As John states, this threefold power group of the *cosmos* is present within me. Every time I let them reign in my life the downsides of Satan's schemes begin to deliver the system's destructive shame and regret.

James recognized our tendencies to cave in to the world system within when he wrote,

> Let no one say when he is tempted, "I am being tempted by God"; for God cannot be tempted by evil, and He Himself does not tempt anyone. But each one is tempted when he is carried away and enticed by his *own* lust. Then when lust has conceived, it gives birth to sin; and when sin is accomplished, it brings forth death. Do not be deceived, my beloved brethren. (1:13–16; italics added)

What does James mean when he speaks of these inner forces? Lusts are legitimate desires that are out of balance or out of bounds. Our flesh is Scripture's way of speaking of our normal physical, emotional, and sensual impulses apart from God in our fallen condition. Our eyes are the windows that connect all that is in the world to the internal systems that control and regulate our behavior. The pride of life are those impulses that drive us to elevate ourselves.

As kingdom pilgrims we feel the tension between serving God and pride in ourselves. The things around us trigger the lusts of our flesh. Our eyes see all that could enhance, empower, and bring pleasure to us, and our self-focused pride reaches out to grab all that will elevate our sense of significance. And the price is merely denying our love and loyalty to God, who has all that this world offers and more in store for us when we get home.

Kingdom pilgrims are pleased with what they have and grateful for what they gain from their love and loyalty to God. And they gladly affirm that there is nothing of value here: The gratification of their flesh, all that their eyes can see, and all that will advance their image, fame, or fortune is not worth trading for their glad allegiance to their King, who is preparing a place for them and who will shower them with uncomparable blessings forevermore in eternity. Kingdom travelers are in this world to serve their King—not themselves or the things this present world offers. They are loyal lovers of the One who is, and all that is eternally ahead for them.

Murphy's Law says, "If anything can go wrong it will." I have a friend who says that O'Toole's Law states that Murphy was an optimist. We live in a fallen place among a fallen race, and, as such, should expect to find our road less than smooth. A trouble-free world is what the world to come is about (Rev. 21:3–5). As the book of Job says, "Man is born for trouble, as sparks fly upward" (Job 5:7). More pointedly Christ warned us, "In the world you have tribulation, but take courage; I have overcome the world" (John 16:33). It is significant that Christ did not say that we *may*, or even that we *will*, have trouble. He simply clarified our expectations by saying, "In the world you *have* tribulation" (italics added). We can expect trouble in every aspect of existence. Trouble is the nature of the new management. There will be trouble with health, careers, children, parents, friends, enemies, finances, cars, houses, plans, dreams, and anything else that finds its way onto the landscape of our lives.

Trouble can come from the material world. Sometimes it comes from the fact that we live among fallen people who trouble us with lying, cheating, gossip, misunderstanding, jealousy, covetousness, envy, anger, temptations that we shouldn't respond to, and expectations that we can't possibly meet. Some of us have deep wounds from living among a fallen race.

To complicate the trouble in this present world, we must remember that we are fallen as well and often make a heap of trouble for ourselves. In the comic strip, Pogo declares: "We have seen the enemy and it is us!" I have to admit that there are days that my own responses are surprising, when I think, say, and do things that are trouble looking for a place to land. I have near out-of-body experiences as I look at myself and say, "Stowell, was that you? . . . Amazing!" As the old spiritual says, "It's not my brother nor my sister but it's me, O Lord, standin' in the need of prayer."

THE TROUBLE IS . . .

But when Christ said that life inevitably involved trouble, He was speaking of the direct conflict that His disciples would experience with the world system as they would live out the righteous principles and practices of the kingdom to come. He noted:

> "These things I have spoken to you, that you may be kept from stumbling. They will make you outcasts from the synagogue, but an hour is coming for everyone who kills you to think that he is offering service to God. And these things they will do, because they have not known the Father, or Me. But these things I have spoken to you, that when their hour comes, you may remember that I told you of them. And these things I did not say to you at the beginning, because I was with you" (John 16:1–4).

He also lets them know that "If the world hates you, you know that it has hated Me before it hated you. If you were of the world, the world would love its own; but because you are not of the world, but I chose you out of the world, therefore the world hates you. Remember the word that I said to you, 'A slave is not greater than his master.' If they persecuted Me, they will also persecute you; if they kept My word, they will keep yours also" (John 15:18–20).

The impact of the world system is coming into full bloom in America. In the past, through nearly all of our history, a blatant expression of the *cosmos* was veiled behind our Christian heritage. The very roots of our society were grounded in the law of Moses and the teachings of Christ. Virtues like honesty, integrity, character, purity, generosity, chastity, kindness, and hard work prevailed. Adultery, homosexuality, greed, and abortion were unthinkable. For nearly everyone, divorce was not an option. Over the last four decades the restraints of our kingdom virtues have been declared out of style, and the absolutes of righteousness are no longer welcome in the public arena.

The trouble for kingdom travelers is that as people of virtues and righteous actions, our very presence is a source of reproof. The light is less than welcome when the world loves darkness. As torchbearers in Sizzleland we have been marginalized by the mainstream of the world system that is now in full control of the American culture. The King has been drummed out of education as secular theories of humanism and evolution explain for students the origin and purpose of life. Music, the media, movies, documentaries, and sitcoms all paint Christians as incompetent, bigoted, nerdish, and thoughtless people. Those of us who live under the kingdom truth are often mocked and avoided by the world at large, and the pressure to conform creates considerable trouble for us.

Fewer things are more unsettling to us than the realization that our righteousness will inevitably cause us to face moments of rejection, discomfort, and in some cases physical pain—and, as many have, even martyrdom.

There is probably no more dramatic moment in Scripture that illustrates how intimidating our identity with the King can be in the face of a hostile environment than the story of Peter around the fire after his Lord had been taken off to the courts and subsequently crucified. As Christ had predicted, this Peter who was so confident in his commitment to Christ failed under the pressure of the *cosmos* when one of the girls around the fire recognized him as one of the followers of Christ. Not wanting to face the pressure, he denied that he knew Christ. For some of us, denial becomes a way of life as we try to live as silent disciples so that no one will know that we are subjects of the King. As we yield to the patterns and practices of the *cosmos*, others of us overtly deny Him in order to fold into the landscape without the stigma of being different. Some of us have denied our identity with the Lord because of pressure from a pagan boss who has asked us to cheat for corporate gain. Others of us have denied Christ by simply failing to embrace the virtues and the behavior of the kingdom.

BEYOND THE TROUBLE

Let's face it, the tension of this world represents a phenomenal pressure. Yet we must constantly encourage each other with the truth that He has called us to be triumphant, not timid. Ours is the victory. Conquest is our privilege. As kingdom people we announce our victory through a bold expression of the kingdom, as we refuse to deny our identity with the King.

When I was young, God gave me the advantage of a great church youth group and friends who were committed to Jesus Christ. I also enjoyed some good friendships with unsaved guys in my neighborhood and at my high school. Our church was planning an evangelistic outreach, and I got the courage to ask one of my high school friends to come. I told him what the evening was going to be like, and he clearly understood that it was a religious event. He told me that he wasn't interested and he didn't want to come. I didn't think much more about it until the next Monday when I saw him standing with several of the popular people in our high school. They were laughing about the fact that I had invited him to this meeting—joking about him needing religion. I heard them say, "He must think you need to be saved!"

I'll never forget how I felt when I walked by them as they laughed. Rejected. I felt a loss of my place in the circle in which I had been previously accepted. At that point it became obvious to me that to be identified with Christ would at times mean that my life would be troubled by rejection.

A P.S. to that event has helped me keep it in perspective. Several weeks later John, the friend I had invited to that Saturday meeting, was killed in a tragic car accident. The whole school was shocked by his sudden death, and my heart was immediately reminded that life is more than what we have in this world. I'm sure John did not laugh as he faced his Creator, and it saddened me that he was not ready. At that point I decided that to be rejected for inviting him to be ready for the world to come was a trade-off I was willing to make, and that I would hopefully be willing to make for the rest of my life. There are gains beyond this present world that are worth the risk of being maligned and rejected. If all we had was this present world, then why would anyone want to face rejection for identifying with the King? But the promise of eternal joy, of belonging to the King in the world to come is a privilege I do not want to deny.

Peggy Noonan was right when she reminded us that this is the short-lived, nasty, brutish world. If all we have is what it offers, then we are most miserable.

What we must remember, however, is that when Christ warned us of the trouble we would face in this world, He wrapped the warning in the fact that we can find peace in Him and confidence in the fact that He has overcome the world. He said, "These things I have spoken to you, that in Me you may have peace. . . . take courage; I have overcome the world" (John 16:33).

Ultimately, in His time, this present world will come to a reckoning as the world to come overtakes this fallen, fading world. We are people of the world to come, and, as such, the triumph of peace is ours even in the midst of trouble. In fact, triumph identifies us as belonging to eternity. It is the mark of the kingdom that can and must find its expression in our lives.

It's not difficult to remind ourselves that this world is a place where we will inevitably experience trouble. We feel the tensions of the world around us and within us on a daily basis. We regularly face the tension of material, sexual, relational, and personal pressures to yield to the pleasures that this fallen planet offers.

Yet Christ our King calls us to *peace* in Him and to a *confidence* that overcomes the pressure and pain of this world. And if peace and confidence are ours then we have nothing to fear and no reason to be discouraged, especially since eternally we will be free from tension and trouble. This present experience is in reality just the adversary's final attempt, in a last gasping effort, to do as much damage as he can before his certain doom.

CHAPTER EIGHTEEN

TRIUMPH

PEACE AND CONFIDENCE
IN THE MIDST OF CHAOS

T he story of Scott and Janet Willis captured the attention of
the secular media like few stories about Christians have in
recent memory. As they expressed confidence in their King, and
their assurance of a payoff in eternity, many in the press talked
about the fact that the Willises were in a state of shock. They
said that this, no doubt, was that first stage of grief called denial, which enabled them to speak of their religious beliefs with
such peace and confidence. So interested was the press that
one of the major news channels in Chicago did a follow-up story four months later, and to its surprise it found that Scott and
Janet were still living with the peace and confidence that had
sustained them those first few days after the accident.

Five months after the tragedy Scott stood at a men's conference here at Moody before fifteen hundred men and told how
his faith had not been shaken and how his heart was as clearly
riveted to his King as before that tragic accident. With tears
streaking his cheeks and his voice shaking, he talked about the
fact that spring was breaking and baseball season was starting

up again. He spoke of how every spring he and his boys would go to the park where the city leagues played, and he would coach them and do all the things that a dad who was proud of his boys would do. He told how he goes to the park now without his boys, how he is still involved in the program. As men all through the auditorium found tears running down their own cheeks, he went on to say, "But I know my boys are better off, because they're at home in heaven." He again affirmed that though their hearts are broken they live with a secured sense of peace that they serve a God who does all things well, who has a purpose and a plan. And that they are willing to submit to what the King of glory deems best.

For all those who doubt and who say that the Willises are simply in a season of denial, they need to know that it was not denial but rather the acceptance of the truth of eternity and a willing submission to the King that enabled them to use this present world as a platform for triumph. Only a confidence grounded in the One who has overcome the world can give such a sure foundation when earthquakes shake our lives. What a powerful testimony to the reality of a conquering King. When the trouble and tension of this world hit its earthbound residents, they have no resource except for disappointment, discouragement, and ultimately despair. When they deny it, it never goes away. But when Christians are riveted to the peace they have in Jesus Christ and the reality of a better world to come, then they have the privilege of demonstrating to a watching world the great privilege of belonging to the King of eternity.

THE LEGACY OF JOB

Job stands as the classic monument to triumph in a troubling world. His pain and sorrow were immeasurable. His wife encouraged him to curse God and die. His friends only made things worse. But Job was unflinching in allegiance to his God. His life was marked by the response, "Though He slay me, I will hope in Him" (Job 13:15).

What Job didn't know was that he was struggling with the inner tension of his pain to prove a point in heaven. Satan had accused God of only being worthy of allegiance, praise, and worship when He "bought mankind off" with good things. This slander of the eternal worth and value of God was to be proven false in one man who would use his place and lot in life on this planet to prove to all the hosts of the universe, both fallen and righteous, that God is worthy regardless.

It was triumph at its best when this present world was at its worst. Job leads all of us who suffer less on the road called conquest, that we too might play our part in the eternal work of the King by announcing the ultimate defeat of the devil himself through each triumphant moment in our lives.

What then enables us to triumph as we seek to live in the peace and confidence of Christ in the midst of the tension and trouble of this present, passing world? When Christ promised the triumph of peace and confidence, He defined the source of this statement, *"These things* I have spoken to you, that *in Me* you may have peace" and confidence (John 16:33; italics added). What are the "these things" that Christ spoke of? This is a reference to all that has gone before in what is known as the Upper Room Discourse, John 13–16, where the resources for a triumphant response in the midst of the tension and trouble around us are listed. There are six reference points that keep us tranquil and victorious. They begin as John 14 opens with Christ confronting the obvious fear and intimidation that the disciples feel at being left alone without Him in what they realize to be an unfriendly environment—an environment that is about to rise and extinguish the One in whom they have placed all of their hope.

MUTUAL SUPPORT

In John 13:34–35, before He addresses their trauma (John 14:1), He commands us to make sure that we love one another. Since the world is obviously marshaled against us, we need to be tightly bonded to each other in a spirit of love and concern. When the pressures of this world begin to overwhelm us, God intended that the community of believers would encourage, comfort, and help one another stay on track for the King. God has not called us to live in isolation here, but to be enfolded into communities where we share a common identity, behavior, and support. This community of belief is guaranteed by its commitment to love one another. And it is by this love and mutual support that we demonstrate that we belong to the victorious King.

Interestingly, one of the key strategies of the adversary is to break the bonds of love in the body of Christ and to sow the seeds of mistrust and envy. He seeks to divide us into isolated segments of one, where he can easily overcome us.

A SAFE AND CERTAIN FUTURE

Second, Christ assures us that we are not abandoned and, in fact, have an assured future beyond this present world. His words in John 14:1–3 ring with the triumph of peace and confidence:

> Let not your heart be troubled; believe in God, believe also in Me. In My Father's house are many dwelling places; if it were not so, I would have told you; for I go to prepare a place for you. And if I go and prepare a place for you, I will come again, and receive you to Myself; that where I am, there you may be also.

After the horrible bombing of the Murrah Federal Building in Oklahoma City, a survivor who was buried in the rubble told of how, immediately after the bombing, a coworker who was free talked to her, touched her, and assured her that she would help her to safety. Just then, hearing that another bomb was about to explode, all the bystanders were evacuated from the area including the one who had been assuring this woman. She was suddenly alone. Fear gripped her heart as the uncertainty of her safety and rescue was compounded by the threat of another explosion. When the danger passed, her friend returned and led the paramedics to her rescue.

With His disciples about to be left alone in a hostile world that might very well annihilate them, Christ gave them the ultimate assurance that He would return and take them safely home where eternally there would be no jeopardy. Christ will certainly take us safely home as well.

SOMETHING TO BELIEVE IN AND OBEY

Then in John 14:7–15 Christ calls His kingdom travelers to a life of unflinching belief in His Father who is in heaven, and a loving obedience that would always guarantee triumph over the temptations that press us across the line of love and loyalty. Philip asked Christ in the midst of this text to show the Father to the disciples, and then they would be satisfied and experience peace. Christ responded that He was the expression of the Father, and that if they had seen Him they had seen the Father; and if they would ask anything of Him the Father would indeed give it to them; and that if they would obey Him and love Him, this would be the key to their relationship with the Father.

If there is no Father, if there is no God in whom we can unflinchingly trust to take us there to heaven and to satisfy throughout eternity, then we will soon lose heart. The fact that Christ is the One who links us directly to the Father of eternity gives us confidence and compels us to loyal obedience. But Christ was leaving to be with His Father. How can we have peace and confidence in the absence of His presence and power?

A PRESENT HELP

Christ went on to speak of the provision of the Holy Spirit in this world, who would be our empowerment when tension and trouble threatened. In fact, Paul reminds us that if we live in the Spirit by yielding to His teachings and following Him everywhere He guides us (Gal. 5:16–25), we will remain safe and secure in the midst of this precarious world (John 14:16–18).

A PLACE TO BELONG

In John 15 Christ speaks of the privilege of abiding in Him like a branch abides in the vine. The branch bears much fruit as a result of that intimate, unhindered relationship where the vine becomes the source of both strength and fruit. Yielding to the Spirit of God is what it means to abide in Christ. As we obey the Spirit we keep the commandments of Christ, as He said: "If you keep My commandments, you will abide in My love; just as I have kept My Father's commandments, and abide in His love" (John 15:10).

PRAYER

Christ goes on to teach His disciples in chapter 16 that a source of peace and confidence will be their willingness to spend time in prayer, seeking God for their needs and petitioning Him for victory. Prayer keeps us in touch with all that is certain and real. In the buffetings of this present world, it is prayer that anchors our hearts to peace and confidence. Paul recognized this when he wrote, "Be anxious for nothing, but in everything by prayer and supplication with thanksgiving let your requests be made known to God. And the peace of God, which surpasses all comprehension, shall guard your hearts and your minds in Christ Jesus" (Phil. 4:6–7).

If our lives do not triumph in peace and confidence, then it would be good for us to check our embrace of these six resources:

- Is my most intimate support system found in the mutual love and encouragement of fellow believers?
- Do I view my experience here through the reality of His return to take me to a safe and satisfying place He has prepared for me?
- Do I possess an unflinching belief in the eternal God that inspires and motivates me to glad obedience?
- Am I sensitive and submissive to the promptings and directives of the Spirit?
- Do I abide in Christ, or is my life characterized by this present world system?
- What's the measure of my prayer life?

It really comes down to a choice of whether my life will be found *in Him* or *in the world*. As He said, He has overcome the world and in Him alone is peace (John 16:33).

THE KING'S PRAYER FOR HIS OWN

At the conclusion of that affirmation of the triumph that is found in the "these things" of chapters 13–16, Christ lifts His face to His Father and prays for His disciples. In His prayer He reiterates the importance of the disciples bonding together against the forces of this world, and then He speaks clearly about the part His Word will play in their triumph amid tension and trouble. In His prayer (John 17) He asks the Father not to take His disciples out of the world but to leave them in the world to do the work of the Father.

It is clear that He wants us to be in the world but not of the world. He does not want us to live in isolation, but rather to be wrapped with the insulation of the Spirit and the Word of God. In fact, Christ prays to His Father, "I have given them Thy word; and the world has hated them, because they are not of the world, even as I am not of the world. I do not ask Thee to take them out of the world, but to keep them from the evil one. They are not of the world, even as I am not of the world. Sanctify them in the truth; Thy word is truth" (John 17:14–17).

To be sanctified is to be set apart for the Father's use. The sanctifying influence in our lives is the Word of God. It is our allegiance to the truth that makes us distinct. It is the truth of God's Word that enables us to see clearly the lies that are so pervasive in the world around us. As we live solely surrendered to God's Word in every area of our lives, we find that we are indeed set apart from the destructive ways of this present world and pliable in the Father's hands.

Where would we know about a world to come if God hadn't given us His Word about that liberating reality? How would we be certain of the conquering kingdom to which we belong if it weren't for God's Word? How would we know that this present world is ruled by the legions of our adversary, who come against us in spiritual warfare to use us as pawns to defame the reputation of our God who created us and who gave His Son for us? How would we have the peace that we are on the side of what is right, and confidence that Christ has overcome the world and is leading us to a better world beyond? How could we withstand the tensions and troubles of this present world if it weren't for His Word?

TRIUMPH

My heart has not been the same ever since Martie and I flew to the depths of the Ecuadorian rain forest and landed in that village of Auca Indians. I had heard of those five brilliant young men: Jim Elliot, Pete Fleming, Roger Youdarian, Ed McCully, and Nate Saint. When I was just a boy, the story of their martyrdom on that beach in the Curaray River filled the news media. Martie and I floated down that river and stood on the beach that was near the location where those men gave their lives for the cause of eternity. All five of them were missionaries, with families, living in the jungle forest. Together they had been moved to reach the savage killer Aucas with the good news of Jesus Christ.

As they set up camp on that beach, they began to build a relationship with three representatives that the tribe sent out to meet them every day. And then one day the tribe sent, instead of their representatives, a killing party who speared all five of them and threw their bodies into the river. The bodies lay there with their blood washing downstream for five days, while their families waited to find out why they hadn't heard from their husbands and fathers. When the news came, not only were their families and other Christians around the world gripped by grief, but a watching world took notice as well. *Life* magazine ran a cover on the tragedy and sent a photographer whose pictures filled the pages of what was then the nation's most well-read periodical. The marines sent a troop to help guarantee the safety of the search party. To earthbound people it was a waste of five young lives and an unnecessary burden to five fatherless families. Through those early months it was hard to believe that Christ had overcome the world. Lives had been wasted, and the Aucas had not been converted. What peace is to be found in that? God had been defeated.

Beelzebub had extinguished the flame of those five lives, but like trick candles on a birthday cake, the testimonies of those lives given for the King of eternity burst into flame again. Hundreds of young people across America said, "I'll go and take their place." And the world mission force was infused with new life that went around the world for the cause of Christ.

Nate Saint's sister and Jim Elliot's wife were invited to come and live in the tribe. And miraculously they went back to the very people who had killed the men they loved. Rachel Saint and Elisabeth Elliot were confident that Christ had overcome the world. They knew that eternity had not been shaken by the death of their brother and husband. To them the cause remained supreme and secure. Soon that village came to know Christ as their Savior.

When our plane landed we were met by brothers and sisters in Christ. Our two pilots, both graduates of the Moody flight school, were standing with us on the beach that day. They pointed to the Indian who had guided our canoe down the river to that landmark place and said of this short, old, loop-eared man, "He was a member of the killing tribe." It was a chilling thought. They went on, "But now he is our brother in Christ."

The head of the killing tribe, the one who speared Nate Saint, is now an old man in the village and a believer in Jesus Christ. Asked what he is going to do when he gets to heaven and meets Nate Saint, he replied, "I'm going to run and throw my arms around Nate Saint and thank him for bringing Jesus Christ to me and my people." He then added that Nate Saint would throw his arms around him as well, and welcome him home.

One of the old women in the tribe tells of how she stood on the hill watching the tribe spear these five kingdom travelers. She says now that as she lifted her eyes to the sky she saw a white-robed throng hovering over that sight. Eternity was waiting to welcome them home. Perhaps they were angels. Perhaps they were the great host of witnesses who in years gone by had found peace not in this world but in their King, ones who believed that Christ had overcome the world and they could therefore give their lives in this world for Him.

Whatever the meaning, one thing is clear: Not even death can daunt the conquering triumph of the King when travelers to eternity are unflinchingly faithful. Regardless.

It is our privilege in a fleeting, falling world to reclaim a passion for what endures by living here in the light of there under the conquering authority of the King.

> And did He die to prove His love?
> And did He rise more pow'rful still?
> And was His rule on earth started there
> Upon Golgotha's tragic hill?
> Bring me my bow of burning gold!
> Bring me my arrows of desire!
> Bring me my spear! O clouds unfold!
> Bring me my Chariot of Fire!
> I will not cease to spread His light:
> My faith a shield, His Word my sword;
> 'Til Christ, my God, is crowned as King,
> And all the earth shall own Him Lord.[1]

NOTES

Chapter 1: Beyond Ourselves

1. Michael A. Lev, "Couple Held on to God in Tragedy," *Chicago Tribune*, 17 November 1994, 1:1.

Chapter 2: In Other Worlds

1. Peggy Noonan, "You'd Cry Too," *Forbes*, 14 September 1992, 65.
2. Fred Catherwood, "Before It's Too Late," *Evangelicals Now;* as quoted in J. I. Packer, "Fear of Looking Forward," *Christianity Today*, 12 December 1994, 13.
3. Ibid.
4. "Sustained in a Tragedy by Faith," *Chicago Tribune*, 18 November 1994, 1:18.
5. Michael A. Lev, "Couple Held on to God in Tragedy," *Chicago Tribune*, 17 November 1994, 1:1, 18.
6. "Sustained in Tragedy," 1:18.

Chapter 3: Balancing Our Worlds

1. "Strange Stories, Amazing Facts of America's Past," *Readers Digest*, 1989, 139.

Chapter 4: Life in the Long View

1. Linda Holland, *Alabaster Doves* (Chicago: Moody, 1995), 55–67. Used by permission.

Chapter 5: Preoccupied with Paradise

1. C. S. Lewis, *The Screwtape Letters* (New York: Macmillan, 1946), 15.
2. John Baillie, *And the Life Everlasting* (London: Oxford Univ. Press, 1936), 15.
3. Alan Richardson and John Bowden, eds., *The Westminster Dictionary of Christian Theology* (Philadelphia: Westminister, 1984), 146.
4. A. J. Conyers, *The Eclipse of Heaven* (Downers Grove, Ill.: InterVarsity, 1992), 78.
5. Ibid., 58.
6. Colleen McDannell and Bernhard Lang, *Heaven: A History* (London: Yale, 1988), 353.

Chapters 6: Why Heaven Seems So Dim

1. Ray B. Brown, ed. *Mark Twain's Quarrel with Heaven* (New Haven, Conn.: College and Univ. Press, 1979), 63–65.
2. Ibid.
3. Peter Kreeft, *Everything You Ever Wanted to Know About Heaven ... But Never Dreamed of Asking* (San Francisco: Ignatius, 1990), 19.
4. Ibid., 19–20.
5. Colleen McDannell and Bernhard Lang, *Heaven: A History* (London: Yale, 1988), 19.
6. Ibid., 20.
7. Kreeft, *Everything You Ever Wanted to Know About Heaven,* 20–21.
8. Karl Rahner, *Theological Investigations*, trans. Ed Quinn (London: Darton, Longman & Todd, 1984), xix.

Chapter 7: Reigniting the Reality

1. Deborah Sharp, "Pilot Swoops Family out of Cuba," *USA Today*, 21 October 1992, 3A.
2. St. Augustine, *The City of God* (New York: Random House, 1950), 432.
3. C. S. Lewis, *Miracles* (New York: Macmillan, 1955), 178–79.
4. Words to "Finally Home" by Don Wyrtzen and L. E. Singer. Copyright © 1971 by Singspiration Music/ASCAP. All rights reserved. Used by permission of Benson Music Group, Inc.
5. Fergus M. Bordewich, "China's Daring Underground of Faith," *Reader's Digest*, August 1991, 34–35.
6. G. K. Chesterton, *Orthodoxy* (Chicago: Thomas More Association, 1985), 99–100.
7. C. S. Lewis, *Mere Christianity* (New York: Macmillan, 1943), 118.

Chapter 8: For Heaven's Sake

1. C. S. Lewis, *Mere Christianity* (New York: Macmillan, 1943), 118.
2. Ibid., 119.
3. Dan McGraw, "The Christian Capitalists," *U.S. News & World Report*, 13 March 1995, 53.
4. Francis A. Schaeffer, *No Little People* (Downers Grove, Ill.: InterVarsity, 1974), 258–71.
5. Eph. 2:19; Heb. 11:13; 1 Peter 2:11.
6. H. Bietenhard, *"Parepidēmos,"* *Dictionary of New Testament Theology* (Grand Rapids, Mich.: Zondervan, 1975), 1:690.
7. Six characteristics of the pilgrim mind-set can be found by studying Heb. 11:13–19. Briefly, the passage shows that as pilgrims: (1) we live here believing God's promises will be fulfilled ultimately in the world to come (v. 13); (2) we readily sense we don't belong on earth, and are seeking the world to come (v. 13); (3) though we could choose to return and live in the earthbound environment from which we were called, we refuse to think backward to what is past (v. 15); (4) we believe nothing here compares to the better country to which we are going, so our affections are set there (v. 15); (5) with our affections on eternity, God is not ashamed to be called our God (v. 15); (6) nothing here is of greater value than our relationship with God, therefore we can be obedient to the point of ultimate sacrifice (vv. 17–19).

Chapter 9: The Habit of Our Hearts

1. C. S. Lewis, *Mere Christianity* (New York: Macmillan, 1943), 104.
2. Jack Canfield and Mark Hansen, *Chicken Soup for the Soul* (Deerfield Beach, Fla.: Health Communications, 1993), 191.
3. John H. Gerstner, *Jonathan Edwards on Heaven and Hell* (Grand Rapids: Baker, 1980), 11.

Chapter 12: Kingdom Privilege

1. Howard Witt and Lisa Anderson, "Many Jarred at Finding Suspect Is an American," *Chicago Tribune*, 23 April 1995, 1:15; and Lisa Anderson, "Now Fear Grips Even Small Towns," *Chicago Tribune*, 20 April 1995, 1:16.
2. Louise Kiernan and Ellen Warren, *Chicago Tribune*, 21 April 1995, 1:16.

Chapter 14: The Kingdom Look

1. Stephen R. Covey, *First Things First* (New York: Simon & Schuster, 1994), 26.
2. Ibid., 52.
3. William Bennett, *The Book of Virtues* (New York: Simon & Schuster, 1993), 14.
4. Gertrude Himmelfarb, *The De-Moralization of Society* (New York: Knopf, 1994), 15.

Chapter 15: Kingdom Perspectives and Practices

1. Adapted from Charles Swindoll, *Improving Your Serve* (Waco, Tex.: Word, 1981), 53–54.

Chapter 18: Triumph

1. William Blake and Bryan Jeffrey Leech, "And All the Earth Shall Own Him Lord," based on "Jerusalem." Copyright ©1982 by Roberton Publications. Used by permission of the publisher, Theodore Presser Company.

Other Books by Joseph Stowell

Perilious Pursuits
The Upside of Down
Shepherding the Church
Kingdom Conflict
Tongue in Check
Following Christ